Taking Shelter

Praise for this book

'Adequate shelter is essential to the well-being of the poor, but housing finance receives far too little focus. This book helps us understand how lower income people strive to improve their housing and shows us how financial systems can be most supportive. It is a much-needed reminder and update.'
Beth Rhyne, Managing Director, Center for Financial Inclusion

'The world's poor, many of whom are excluded from formal finance, struggle daily to finance adequate housing for their families. This much-needed book both explains and demonstrates how the financial system is providing more options than ever, and what more can be done. Any banker, policy maker, or NGO worker concerned with affordable housing in emerging markets will find practical advice here.'
Amolo Ng'weno, Chief Executive Officer, BFA Global

'Good, quality housing is the foundation on which families build their future. Its absence is one of the mainstays of poverty. As this book rightly points out, enabling families to invest in their homes should be a key objective of financial service providers, and it should be on the must-read list of anyone seeking to better the lives of the poor through financial inclusion.'
Laura Foose, Executive Director, Social Performance Task Force

'This very readable book presents a thorough situation analysis combined with success stories and updated research that will help investors and policy-makers to design and deliver new programs to meet the needs of low income families around the world.'
Debbie Erb, international housing finance expert

'As a funder and practitioner of affordable housing it can be difficult to cut through all the noise and find the signal. *Taking Shelter* does just that. It's hard to put into words the value this book holds for all anyone focused on affordable housing for the base of the pyramid. I'm excited for others to get their hands on this book.'
Matthew Marshall, Co-founder/Head of Product at New Story

'This is a seminal collection of knowledge, experience and thoughts on how to address the burgeoning crisis in housing for the poor.'
Sanjay Sinha, Managing Director, M-CRIL

'While housing financing systems focus on the middle and high-end markets, most of the world's population finance their housing informally, independently, and inefficiently. Making housing markets work for the poor will require the attention of policy makers, regulators and the providers of finance; and the development of financial tools that engage with the realities and capacities of low-income people. *Taking Shelter* offers an important contribution to what must become a critical area of focus as nations grapple with the persistent challenge of affordable housing.'
Kecia Rust, Executive Director, Centre for Affordable Housing Finance in Africa

Taking Shelter
Housing Finance for the World's Poor

Edited by
Patrick McAllister and Daniel Rozas

**Practical
ACTION
PUBLISHING**

Practical Action Publishing Ltd
27a, Albert Street, Rugby,
Warwickshire, CV21 2SG, UK
www.practicalactionpublishing.com

A catalogue record for this book is available from the British Library.
A catalogue record for this book has been requested from
the Library of Congress.

978-178853-034-7 Paperback
978-178853-033-0 Hardback
978-178044-780-3 Epub
978-178044-768-1 PDF

Citation: McAllister, P. and Rozas, D. (2020) *Taking Shelter: Housing Finance
for the World's Poor,* Rugby, UK: Practical Action Publishing
<http://dx.doi.org/10.3362/9781780447681>.

Since 1974, Practical Action Publishing has published and disseminated
books and information in support of international development work
throughout the world. Practical Action Publishing is a trading name
of Practical Action Publishing Ltd (Company Reg. No. 1159018), the
wholly owned publishing company of Practical Action. Practical Action
Publishing trades only in support of its parent charity objectives and any
profits are covenanted back to Practical Action (Charity Reg. No. 247257,
Group VAT Registration No. 880 9924 76).

Cover Credit: RCO.design
Cover image credit: UN-Habitat/Julius Mwelu
Typeset by vPrompt eServices, India

Contents

Figures, tables, boxes and stories

Figures

Tables

Boxes

Stories

Acronyms

ADB	Asian Development Bank
AFD	Agence Française de Développement
AHF	affordable housing finance
A-HFC	affordable housing finance company
Bps	basis points
CAMEL	capital, asset quality, management, earnings, liquidity
CERSAI	Central Registry of Securitisation, Asset Reconstruction and Security Interest of India
CLSS	credit linked subsidy scheme
CPSD	country private sector diagnostic
DFI	development finance institution
DFHL	Dewan Finance Housing Limited
DFID	Department for International Development
EMA	European Microfinance Award
EWS	economically weaker section
e-MFP	European Microfinance Platform
FMV	Fondo Mi Vivienda
FSP	financial service provider
GDP	gross domestic product
GHG	greenhouse gas
GIIN	Global Impact Investment Network
GRIHA	Green Rating for Integrated Habitat Assessment
HKL	Hattha Kaksekar Limited
HMF	housing microfinance
HOFINET	Housing Finance Network
IAY	Indira Awas Yojina
IFC	International Finance Corporation
IFIF	India Financial Inclusion Fund
IGBC	Indian Green Building Council
IMGC	India Mortgage Guarantee Corporation
IPO	initial public offering
LIG	lower income group
LP	limited partner
MFI	microfinance institution
MHFC	Micro Housing Finance Corporation
MIG	middle income group
MIV	microfinance investment vehicle
MSME	micro, small and medium enterprise

NBFC	non-bank financial company
NHB	National Housing Bank
NIM	net interest margin
OPIC	Overseas Private Investment Corporation
PMAY	Prime Minister's Housing Programme
PPP	purchasing power parity
PSL	priority sector lending
RBI	Reserve Bank of India
RERA	Real Estate Regulation and Development Act
RHISS	Rural Housing Interest Subsidy Scheme
SACCO	saving and credit co-operative
SDG	Sustainable Development Goals
SFB	small finance bank
TA	technical assistance

Foreword

Shelter is a basic human need intertwined with safety and security, food, hygiene, education, gender empowerment, and asset building. At the same time, finance that makes quality housing both accessible and affordable is a key building block of social and economic development. Our organizations have spent the past decade and more developing and supporting innovations in affordable housing finance. Yet its role within the inclusive finance sector has remained stunted even as growing populations, economic growth, and urbanization have created more demand for affordable housing. Now is the time for the supply to match that demand, and *Taking Shelter: Housing Finance for the World's Poor* shows how this can be done.

Microfinance for Housing was the topic of the European Microfinance Award (EMA) in 2017 – and a major focus of the e-MFP-hosted European Microfinance Week that year. The clear enthusiasm and buy-in we saw among stakeholders for a re-invigorated focus on this subject was instrumental in the realization of this book. Discussions began about how, despite the fascinating innovations profiled in that year's EMA, there was no single place where the best practices could be consolidated; no 'one-stop-shop' for information on the need, the challenges, and the solutions to scaling up housing microfinance to meet the housing finance needs of over a billion people worldwide. We all immediately saw the value of this project, and *Taking Shelter* is the output of almost three years of coordinated activity to produce a defining text on the subject.

It was an enormously ambitious idea, and we believe that it has produced an outstanding piece of work. Expertly edited by Patrick McAllister and Daniel Rozas, the book brings together contributions from the leading thinkers and practitioners in housing microfinance. It takes any reader, from neophyte to expert, on a journey through the complex network of the housing microfinance ecosystem. Grounded in the reality of the world's poor, *Taking Shelter* shows where the sector can – and we believe must – go from here.

We are proud to have played our role in shepherding this book through those early conceptual discussions, selecting chapters and authors, and the enormous editing job that led to this finished work. We hope its publication is not the end of this long process, but instead heralds a new impetus to ensure that, one day, everyone in the world will have access to affordable, quality housing – and the financial services to make that dream possible.

Lucie Astier-Such, Agence Française de Développement
Alex Silva, Calmeadow
Laura Hemrika, Credit Suisse
Patrick Kelley, Habitat for Humanity International
Claudia Rojas, Triple Jump

Foreword: implications of the Covid-19 pandemic

Already in 2019, as the authors were writing this book, the sheer scale of housing needed over the coming decades, and the investment needed to finance it, were daunting. The global slum population was already estimated at 1 billion and expected to double by 2030 (UN-Habitat, 2016). This crisis prompted housing to be included in the update to the Millennium Development Goals and in 2015 the World agreed to Sustainable Development Goal 11 – Sustainable Cities and Communities. A specific target on housing was set: 'By 2030, ensure access for all to adequate, safe and affordable housing and basic services and upgrade slums'. Although some countries such as India, Kenya and Pakistan have made housing improvement a priority, it has by no means been a universal policy imperative. The authors could not have foreseen what 2020 was to bring.

The Covid-19 pandemic has affected all aspects of society but has had the deepest impact on those most vulnerable who were already living precarious existences with uncertain incomes and limited capacity to withstand natural disasters. Although much remains to be understood about the impact of Covid-19, direct linkages have been made between housing conditions, poverty and the prevalence of this coronavirus. Indeed, the pandemic has been characterized as a 'housing disease' at times. An article published towards the beginning of the pandemic included a chart showing a clear correlation between death levels from Covid-19 in the United Kingdom and the level of overcrowded housing (Barker, 2020). Almost the same chart has been produced by the Public Policy Institute of California, with the added dimension that essential workers are much more likely to be living in some of that over-crowded housing (Mejia and Cha, 2020). It is likely that these findings will be replicated and re-affirmed in emerging economies where over-crowding and poor quality housing is the daily reality for large swathes of the population. The links between good housing, sanitation and health had always been well understood, so this pandemic is a further reminder of the vital role that adequate housing can play in ensuring wellbeing.

In 2018, the World Health Organization published *Housing and Health Guidelines*. They state boldly that 'improved housing conditions can save lives, prevent disease, increase quality of life, reduce poverty and help mitigate climate change'. This message is more relevant than ever. The links between health and housing can be seen on multiple levels ranging from good construction and adherence to codes through to issues such as proper ventilation and heating. Sub-standard housing which is difficult to heat or not well insulated can contribute to poor respiratory or cardio-vascular outcomes. Another common problem, especially in emerging economies, is dirt floors which not only create breeding grounds for mosquitoes to then transmit diseases such as malaria but also increase the likelihood of diarrhea contraction. All of these effects compromise immune systems and increase the likelihood and severity of infection from viruses, including Covid-19. The solution is often straightforward and may simply require a small loan to install a concrete floor, or to improve a home by better insulating it. Mexico's famous *Piso Firme*, literally meaning firm floor, was rolled out in 2000 with the objective of replacing dirt floors with concrete. The programme was a mixture of government support and loans, and reached millions of households, significantly improving health outcomes (Cattaneo et al., 2009). Small amounts of financing to improve housing can have literally life-changing impacts.

A further aspect of the pandemic that is still unfolding is on the housing finance side, with increasing risks of potentially deep and long-lasting economic damage. The World Bank prepared a quick briefing note as the world geared up to better understand and combat the effects of Covid-19 on multiple fronts. One of the concerns highlighted was that as households are confined to home and unemployment increases, there will be wave of defaults on housing loans or on rents. Landlords and mortgage lenders have introduced widespread programmes of moratoria to stave off the immediate impact, in the hope of a V-shaped recovery. At some point towards the end of 2020, the moratoria will come to an end and longer-term solutions will have to be envisaged by the financial sector, property investors, households and public authorities. We learned a great many lessons in the aftermath of the financial crisis and the sub-prime crisis. One lesson in particular, was that those on lower incomes are often the worst affected with limited financial safety nets to fall back on. In the current crisis, there is an opportunity to pre-empt some of the worst effects which were seen in the wake of the 2009 global financial crisis. Measures can be taken now to guard against mass waves of defaults, and collapsing property markets, leading to a liquidity squeeze in the banking system and a freezing up of capital markets. Policy makers and central banks generally have taken a much more pro-active response in responding to the crisis, but there may yet be some distance to go.

Many of the effects described above relate more to developed economies, which benefit from active capital markets and may be more susceptible to financial shocks. However the risk in developing economies is that burgeoning housing finance systems and institutions that are just beginning to have an impact and deliver housing investment could face an uncertain future, potentially setting back development efforts that have been underway for many years in some cases. So although the total financial exposure may be more manageable in many emerging economies, the lasting damage to housing finance systems could be much more severe. This implies the need for continued support to sustain liquidity for financial institutions and resolution mechanisms that do not deplete capital resources from the financial system. At the same time, one cannot forget the human dimension of borrowers who have lost income and may be struggling to meet repayment obligations.

The extent of the global economic slowdown resulting from Covid-19, the scale of unemployment and the impact on the financial system are still difficult to predict at this stage. In some countries we are already witnessing a resumption of normal economic life and activity. A rapidly rebounding housing sector can play a vital role in reviving economic growth and job markets. This is especially true in emerging economies where job multipliers for housing are higher due to higher reliance on labour. It is worth remembering that in the US following the Great Depression one of the key parts of the New Deal was a set of measures focusing on stimulus for housing construction as a means to boost economic activity. It is often the case that new initiatives are borne out of times of crisis. A 'Housing New Deal' addressing the ambitious targets of SDG11 and the commitments made at Habitat III could be a positive outcome which helps heal some of the damage of the Covid-19 pandemic.

Aside from the current Covid-19 crisis another dynamic has been at play in the affordable housing sector over the past few years. We have been witnessing a shift towards much more market-based solutions aiming to be more scalable and sustainable. The concept of housing microfinance was introduced with all the promise and expectation of delivering the rapid solutions that made microfinance such a success in areas such as microenterprise development. However, one of the major differences was that the traditional microfinance loan which follows the short-term cashflows of a micro or small business carries much more risk when it is extended over a longer period to accommodate a housing loan. Additionally, many of the security mechanisms applied to traditional microfinance such as group guarantees become much less reliable and effective when stretched over much longer periods and applied in an urban context where the social fabric is not as strong. Numerous attempts have been made to launch housing microfinance pilots with the objective of demonstrating the viability of the product. Many of them did result in impressive results but were also heavily reliant on either subsidized funding or technical assistance support. So, while good results can be achieved, it is debatable whether scaling up can be done without additional non-market resources to provide additional support. How can larger scale capital market resources be mobilized if grant funding or additional technical assistance is also required – and should this not also be priced in?

A mixed solution which incorporates some of the elements of financial access and outreach of microfinance with the more hard-nosed commercial practices in mortgage lending began to emerge. The Affordable Housing Institute promoted a mantra of underwriting informality and investing in market-based solutions. It followed through on rhetoric with actions and invested in SEWA Grih Rin in India, now called Sitara. It is part of the SEWA network which focuses on supporting Self Employed Women. The values of Sitara are to provide affordable housing finance to the underserved and informally employed. It does so in a very business-orientated way, whereas in the past solutions may have been more focused on a grants-based approach which limits sustainability over the long term and also limits capacity to scale up and reach the millions who need housing finance.

A similar change in approach can be seen with Habitat for Humanity, as described in Chapter 4. The Terwilliger Center for Innovation in Shelter is one of Habitat for Humanity's main initiatives and has clearly set out guiding principles which include 'Strive for scale to reach many families' and 'sustainability'. The latter principle is defined as the provision of lasting solutions where costs can be covered and some profit can be earned. Furthermore, there is a focus on avoidance of market distortions and a 'positive attitude' to private sector involvement.

The key change in thinking in these cases was the need for sustainability and for scale to match the growing level of demand. As is often the case in development, the change in thinking on housing microfinance also coincided with rapid technological changes in the way housing loans are underwritten, monitored and financed. Advancements in data analysis, in loan servicing and administration, higher data storage and transfer capacity all brought down the cost of administering housing loans. There can now be a level of scrutiny and risk analysis of a borrower's repayment capacity that would have been unthinkable just a few years ago. At that time, the overhead costs of processing a housing loan and trying to secure collateral meant that small loan sizes were effectively uneconomic, but this is no longer the case. Fully integrated CRM platforms have removed the need for heavy investment into branch networks, and businesses are fully scalable with IT resources matching exact capacity required. Loan officers are mobile, armed with tablets and apps able to deal with dialects or illiteracy, and fully connected to credit databases. They can now verify collateral and provide rapid access to long-term housing loans.

This book represents a much-needed update at what may be seen as an inflection point in terms of the provision of access to affordable housing finance. Housing needs are still rising and the Covid-19 pandemic has brought an even greater urgency to the universal provision of adequate, safe and affordable housing. Reaching those on lower incomes is a necessity if the SDG11 target on housing is to be met. The scale of investment required cannot come from government or donor resources alone. Long-term resources from capital markets will be required which in turn implies the need for economically viable lending models. The challenge is enormous but, equally, the welfare, economic and social benefits have the potential to be transformative.

Simon Walley, Lead Financial Sector Specialist, World Bank

References

Barker, N. (2020) 'The housing pandemic: four graphs showing the link between COVID-19 deaths and the housing crisis', Inside Housing, 29 May 2020 <https://www.insidehousing.co.uk/insight/the-housing-pandemic-four-graphs-showing-the-link-between-covid-19-deaths-and-the-housing-crisis-66562> [last accessed 30 September 2020]

Cattaneo, Matias D., Sebastian Galiani, Paul J. Gertler, Sebastian Martinez, and Rocio Titiunik (2009) 'Housing, health, and happiness', *American Economic Journal: Economic Policy*, 1 (1): 75–105. doi: 10.1257/pol.1.1.75

Mejia, M.C. and Cha, P. (2020) 'Overcrowded housing and COVID-19 risk among essential workers' Public Policy Institute of California, May 2020, <https://www.ppic.org/blog/overcrowded-housing-and-covid-19-risk-among-essential-workers/> [last accessed 30 September 2020]

UN-Habitat (2016) 'Slum Almanac 2015-16: Tracking Improvement in the Lives of Slum Dwellers', UN-Habitat [last accessed 30 September 2020]

WHO (2018) *Housing and Health Guidelines* <https://www.who.int/publications/i/item/who-housing-and-health-guidelines> [last accessed 30 September 2020]

World Bank (2020) 'COVID-19 Outbreak: Housing finance implications and response' http://pubdocs.worldbank.org/en/368571586473125247/COVID-19-Outbreak-Housing-Finance.pdf [last accessed 30 September 2020]

Editors' preface

You know that you have arrived in your field of specialization when people start asking you to recommend books on the topic. We have been confidently recommending *Housing Microfinance: A Guide to Practice* by Frank Daphnis and Bruce Ferguson for years. However, by 2016 the book had been doing service for over 10 years. Housing microfinance had gone from being a niche product for a small number of microfinance institutions to a significant part of the loan book of some large institutions. Financing available for the housing portion of lending portfolios was also changing as private equity and debt investors joined development finance institutions (DFIs) and bilateral assistance organizations as key funders of microfinance. Microfinance itself was expanding beyond the confines of NGOs to more commercially oriented institutions that could reach larger numbers and a broader range of customers. Some of them were also going beyond microfinance into secured lending and mortgage finance. Regulators were considering the impact all this would have, both on the financial system and on individual customers entrusting their savings and livelihoods to these institutions.

It was around this time that we began thinking something more was needed. We both come from mortgage backgrounds but had migrated to microfinance, and we were beginning to see that these lines were blurring. We felt a new book was needed to explain how housing microfinance had evolved into a more hybrid way to finance housing for the world's poor.

Over coffee at e-MFP's annual European Microfinance Week, a plan was hatched. After conferring with several leaders in housing and microfinance to confirm our hunch that a new book was needed, we asked e-MFP to sponsor the book, and thankfully they agreed. Next, we lined up a small amount of funding to get started and found Practical Action Publishing, which was willing to take a chance on us. Finally, at the next European Microfinance Week, we began to approach authors we knew would have insight into the topic.

Over the course of two years we gathered and edited the chapters and formed strong bonds with the authors. We learned more than we taught and leaned heavily on our families and colleagues while we devoted our spare time to this project. The result is what we hope is a book that speaks to anyone interested in the topic of housing finance for the world's poor. If you are reading this, that's you. We hope you find it as instructive to read as it was to edit.

Patrick McAllister, Washington, DC
Daniel Rozas, Brussels

Acknowledgements

First and foremost, the editors would like to thank the authors who are all leaders in the field. They were not compensated but nevertheless spent hours writing these chapters under deadline, responding to all our queries, incorporating edits, updating data, and doing it all with good cheer. This book is mostly a compendium of their experiences in the world of housing finance and we were lucky to have been able to work with them.

This book would not have been possible without the support of Christoph Pausch and the team at e-MFP, the book's administrative home, including Niamh Watters who oversaw all the photos and Camille Dassy who greatly improved the graphics in chapter 2.

We had early support from the funders who showed their appreciation in the most concrete way possible! A very special thanks to Alex Silva of Calmeadow, who agreed to underwrite a major part of the book, and to Credit Suisse, the Terwilliger Center for Innovation in Housing at Habitat for Humanity International, Triple Jump, and Agence Française de Développement. In a short time they came through with the funding needed to get started.

Our thanks to Bruce Ferguson who generously shared his experiences and gave us his thoughts on what a new book on this topic should cover.

We would also like to thank: Olivia Nielsen for her explanation of how people build (box 3.1); Amelia Greenberg for her insights on the social impact of housing; Sam Mendelson for his input on microfinance for WASH and energy (Chapter 2); and Maria Teresa Morales for her explanation of regulations encouraging housing finance in Bolivia (Box 2.2). Thanks also to R.V. Verma and Mona Kachhwaha who both provided material pertaining to India in Chapter 2.

Beth Rhyne is owed special gratitude for reviewing the entire manuscript and guiding us to some much needed improvements. Our chapter reviewers Bezant Chonga, Pam Hedstrom, Laura Hemrika, Camilla Nestor, Tim Ogden, and M.S. Sriram read and commented on drafts of the chapters. Frank Pichel of Cadasta reviewed sections related to land policy.

Chapter 3 author Stuart Rutherford wrote the introductory paragraphs and the case studies from the Hrishipara Daily Diary Project in Bangladesh. The editors supplied the remaining case studies and some material in the later part of the chapter, and Rutherford would like to acknowledge both them and the sources of their case studies.

Chapter 4 authors Sandra Prieto and Patrick Kelley drew on years of experience as consultants and at Habitat for Humanity International and its Terwilliger Center for Innovation in Shelter, where numerous people have contributed to their years of learning. Special names to call out include external consultant contributions, namely: Carter Garber, Kecia Rust, Bill Allison, and Christy Stickney.

Introduction

If one were to ask people around the world to name their three largest expenses, housing would nearly always feature at the top of that list. Housing is the first, along with food and water, of the hierarchy of human needs as famously described by the psychologist Abraham Maslow in 1943. But unlike those other basic needs, reliable shelter requires long-term investment. Turning small, frequent cashflows into the large amount needed to make such an investment is one of the main functions of financial services.

Improving housing is one of the most direct means available to reduce poverty and advance other social objectives. This is why the Progress Out of Poverty Index, a mainstay of poverty measurement in the financial inclusion sector, uses observations on housing (type of building materials, number of rooms, on-site access to clean water and sanitation), among others, to determine poverty levels (IPA, 2020).[1] By improving sanitation and reducing indoor air pollution, improved housing directly contributes to improved health, which has taken on a new urgency with the arrival of the Covid-19 pandemic. It gives children the physical space they need for study, thereby improving education outcomes. When combined with appropriate rights of ownership, housing can also be a major factor in increasing the financial and social independence of women. These are just a few of the many benefits of decent housing.

In the global South, the poor face major housing challenges due to both rapid urbanization and the poor quality of existing housing. This suggests that housing finance for the world's poor should be a major focus of financial providers: it helps households meet a basic need, does so by fulfilling a primary role of financial services, and faces huge levels of demand worldwide. Among the many actors in the inclusive finance community, however, only a minority see housing finance as a key area of interest (Mendelson, 2019).[2] Perhaps this is due to the complexity of housing finance, which requires at least a basic understanding of the government policies that set the foundation on which a country's housing finance system rests, and the diverse array of funding types: government, private, and development investors providing debt and equity investment, all with various risk mitigants, credit enhancements, and incentives. Lenders entering this market must also develop an understanding of building practices and construction materials, land policy and legal tenure, urban planning, provision of utilities and services, and, perhaps most importantly, the aspirations and capabilities of poor households that more often than not build their own homes. All this is in addition to the already substantial complexity of providing financial services to poor borrowers with informal incomes and few, if any, assets.

http://dx.doi.org/10.3362/9781730447681.001

Even so, over the past two decades the housing finance ecosystem has been growing and evolving. A dedicated group of specialist organizations have maintained a steadfast focus on housing finance, developing a set of practices and building experiences that are both replicable and scalable. Today, there are more institutions working with poor clients, more investors that provide funding, and more policy-makers setting an appropriate enabling environment for affordable housing finance.

This book presents the experiences of these key actors in order to describe how housing finance can be an effective solution to the housing challenges of the world's poor.

Chapter 1: *The global housing finance challenge for the underserved* by Marja Hoek-Smit examines the scale of the challenge. While poverty has seen major declines in the past few decades, many families, even those whose earnings put them above the national poverty line, continue to live in substandard housing. Moreover, while housing finance is a mainstay of retail financial markets in wealthy countries, it remains small in middle-income countries and minimal in the poorest ones. The chapter further introduces the two main types of housing finance – mortgage and housing microfinance – and examines the advantages and opportunities of each approach in meeting the housing needs of the poor.

Chapter 2: *The housing finance ecosystem for the world's poor* by Daniel Rozas and Patrick McAllister takes the full measure of the complexity of the housing ecosystem. It begins with its core foundations: land, building, and finance. The section on land briefly examines the laws and policies surrounding land ownership, tenure, title, and cadaster. The building section presents an overview of the building codes and services that underpin materials, building norms, know-how, roads, and utilities that determine the type of housing and communities that will evolve. The finance section delves into the multiple layers of housing finance, from the financial practices of the households to the financial providers (including the informal sector) that support housing, to the multiple actors that provide investment and funding, and to the enabling environment created by government policies and regulations. The chapter concludes with a case study of the housing finance sector in India and the key elements that have shaped its evolution.

Chapter 3: *Do-it-yourself housing* by Stuart Rutherford explores how poor households plan and finance the building of their own homes, from their own perspective. Drawn from a series of financial diaries and other stories, these home builders from Bangladesh to Nicaragua show how poor households use *housing as a verb*: living in ever changing, evolving structures that they build, expand, and improve as the needs of the family grow and resources become available. Many of them finance the building entirely from the informal financial sector, while others combine both microfinance and informal finance to expand their homes over many months and years.

Chapter 4: *Housing microfinance* by Sandra Prieto and Patrick Kelley shows how the clients presented in Chapter 3 aggregate into demand for housing microfinance and how microfinance institutions (MFIs) have successfully incorporated housing products into their loan portfolios. Building on over a decade of experience working with dozens of MFIs, the authors examine how housing microfinance differs from traditional microfinance lending and how it is evolving from a niche product for the most successful clients into a product line that attracts new clients. The chapter also briefly explores the business case for housing microfinance and the role of non-financial services.

Chapter 5: *The funding landscape for affordable housing finance*, by multiple authors, shares their experiences funding the institutions that provide affordable housing, as well as highlighting the limitations of the current market. The chapter presents impact investors managing debt and equity funds, development finance institutions (both bi- and multi-lateral), government-affiliated local housing investment funds, and even a brief foray into funding opportunities from the capital markets and securitization. Together, these cases provide a broad overview of the roles of different investors and how, collectively, they play a fundamental role in building an effective housing finance sector that can serve the needs of poor households.

The book closes with a look at the trends and challenges that should define the evolution of housing finance in the years to come. The future it envisions is less a prognosis and more a call to action for the many stakeholders that make up the sector.

Demand for housing will continue to grow. This book provides the stakeholders that make up the inclusive finance sector – from providers to investors to policy-makers – with lessons and examples to build and scale an effective housing finance sector. All that's left is to seize the opportunity to change the lives of hundreds of millions around the world.

Notes

1. A sample of country indexes shows 2–3 household-related indicators are typically included in a 10-indicator scorecard.
2. The respondents to this survey of inclusive finance actors ranked housing microfinance 8th out of 15 new areas of focus.

References

IPA (2020) *Poverty Probability Index*, Innovations in Poverty Action, New Haven, CT <www.povertyindex.org> [accessed May 2020].

Mendelson, S. (2019) *The Financial Inclusion Compass 2019*, e-MFP, Luxembourg.

CHAPTER 1

The global housing finance challenge for the underserved

Marja C. Hoek-Smit

Housing finance systems, both housing microfinance and mortgage systems, need to be scaled up, specifically in developing economies, to address the growing pressure on the affordable housing sector, driven by urbanization and growing environmental risks. While in advanced economies residential mortgages have long been the dominant type of household credit, in developing economies mortgage lending has stagnated as a percentage of total household credit over the past decades and housing microfinance is still very small in scale. Access to finance for affordable rental housing, whether through mortgage or microfinance, is mostly absent. These are major concerns. Both types of housing finance are needed to leverage household savings and private sector funds to improve the housing conditions of the underserved populations – poor and not so poor, informally and formally employed, and those with different types of tenure, types of collateral, and property rights.

Keywords: housing microfinance; mortgage finance; affordable housing; housing-finance market integration; credit market scale over time; financialization

A broad segment of the population in low- and middle-income countries suffers from inadequate housing. Not just the very poor or informally employed but also low-income households in the formal workforce. Pressure on the affordable housing sector will dramatically increase during the coming decades both for new housing and the improvement of existing housing, particularly in urban areas. The causes vary across cities and countries, and require, therefore, different types of solutions. This will involve shifts in fundamental housing supply elements that will take time to implement: land regulations and management, density regulations and building techniques, and transportation systems. One thing is clear, however: household savings and private-sector funds need to be leveraged to improve housing demand and supply, and housing finance mechanisms play a key role in that process. The days of looking at housing finance for the world's underserved populations as a small niche market are fading rapidly.

http://dx.doi.org/10.3362/9781780447681.002

Financial sector trends and challenges

Globally, credit to the private sector has increased dramatically over the past decades, relative to the size of national economies. Household credit has been responsible for most of this growth, and more specifically so in developing economies according to a recent study (Muller, 2018).[1,2] Lending to the corporate sector, including small and medium enterprise (SME) lending, has only just kept up with economic growth in high-income countries over the past 35 years, and has in fact decreased relative to economic growth in low income countries between 1980 and the mid-2000s.[3] But how much of the enormous growth in household credit benefited the world's poor, and what fraction of household credit was used for housing?

The Global Findex Data Base survey, conducted every other year by the World Bank Group, provides the most comprehensive demand-side picture of the use of global financial services with a focus on financial inclusion. The most recent survey (2017) shows that approximately 50 per cent of adults borrowed money in the past year, in line with the growing household credit findings in the Muller study (World Bank, 2018a). In advanced economies, over 60 per cent of adults borrowed; the great majority from formal financial institutions. In developing economies meanwhile, just over 40 per cent borrowed, mostly from family or friends. In general, and not surprisingly, higher status groups (e.g. the richest 60 per cent, and those with secondary education), have a higher propensity to borrow.

In terms of housing lending, in high-income countries residential mortgages have made up a relatively stable fraction of 60 to 70 per cent of household credit since the 1950s with a peak during the housing boom of the 2000s.[4] By contrast, in developing economies the share of residential mortgages in household lending has decreased over the past decades and today is an average of 40 per cent.[5] In fact the largest and most rapidly increasing proportion of household credit in developing economies is made up of consumer credit (55 per cent of total household credit today) followed by credit card loans and car loans (Muller, 2018).

Data from the Housing Finance Information Network (HOFINET) confirm the discrepancy in size of the mortgage market relative to GDP between advanced and developing economies (Figure 1.1). In some countries, such as South Africa, mortgage lending relative to GDP has in fact declined in the last decade, despite, or maybe as a result of, low GDP growth.

Data on the size of the housing microfinance market are not systematically collected. The best source of data on housing microfinance is the annual survey of microfinance institutions by Habitat for Humanity, which is discussed in some detail in Chapter 4 (Habitat for Humanity, 2017). Its 2016–17 survey showed the still nascent, but growing, state of the sector: in 70 per cent of the microfinance institutions in the survey the total housing loan portfolio was USD 5 million or less. While that is most certainly an underestimation of the total microloans used for housing (an estimated

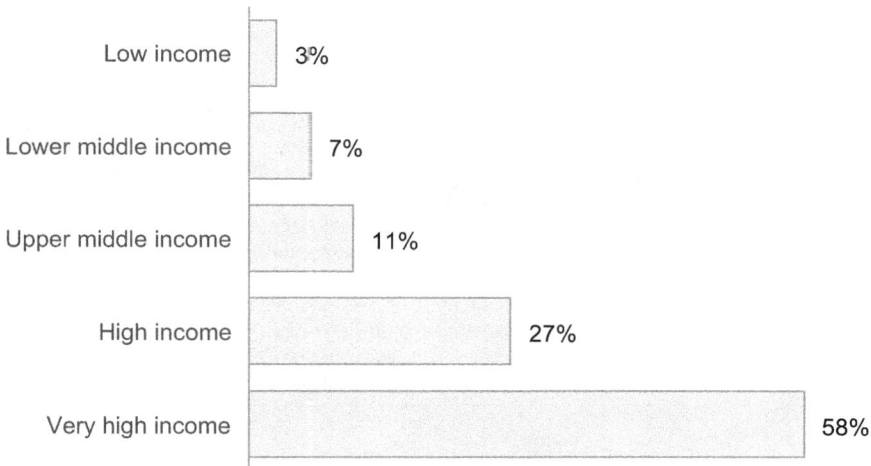

Figure 1.1 Mortgage debt to GDP by income level of country[6]
Source: Housing finance information network HOFINET www.hofinet.org

10 to 20 per cent of total MSME loans is reportedly used for housing), these figures show the small scale of the sector.[7]

The Findex survey data on users of credit show a similar small scale of exposure to housing loans in their survey. It finds that in advanced economies an average of 27 per cent of adults had an outstanding housing loan in the past year, including mortgage and non-mortgage loans for housing, while in developing countries this figure was below 10 per cent.

Given the enormous requirement for new housing and home improvements in developing countries, the small size of the housing finance sector is worrisome. Mortgage credit is the cheapest form of credit available in most countries because the use of property collateral reduces the credit risk for the lender, at least in efficient mortgage systems. The property and credit information systems needed to expand the primary mortgage market typically improve with overall economic and financial sector growth and open up the use of capital market funding for housing finance.[8] Recent private sector innovations and strategic government policies in several developing countries have sped up this process, but need to be much more broadly adopted (see Chapter 5 for an exploration of capital market funding).

By contrast, housing microfinance, which does not require a lien on the property and mostly uses soft collateral or guarantees, would appear to have fewer constraints to reaching scale and, particularly, to reaching underserved segments of the housing market.[9] However, the lack of enforceable collateral makes these loans more risky for lenders. Because of this risk, housing microfinance loans carry higher interest rates than mortgage loans, which limits the demand for those products. Also, non-collateralized loans are typically much smaller than mortgage loans and have a shorter loan term. As described in detail in Chapter 4,

---

Box 1.1 The financialization debate

The swift growth in the mortgage sector in some advanced economies before the global financial crisis and the high levels of defaults and foreclosures that occurred when the housing bubble burst, is frequently associated with subprime mortgage lending to households with low and unstable incomes and poor credit records. This perception generated negative views about the 'financialization' of housing and the dangers of housing finance for lower income populations globally (Schularick & Taylor 2012).[10] Such views have proven to be misleading, but can nevertheless initiate public policy decisions that discourage access to housing finance for underserved households (Ferreria 2018, Albanesi et al., 2017, Ferreira et al., 2015).[11]

More importantly, financialization of housing has not been an issue in developing economies. Rather, housing finance in these countries is still in very short supply and is badly needed to address housing shortages, in particular for households with low or informal incomes and without officially recognized land titles.

---

microfinance loans for housing are still used mostly for incremental building or home improvements, and, to a limited degree, for home extensions with rental units. Moreover, appropriate expandable and affordable housing options are in short supply in most growing cities in developing countries, further limiting demand for the housing microfinance product. These supply and demand constraints are the focus of the remaining chapters in this book.

In summary, growth in household credit has been responsible for most of the dramatic global credit growth in the private sector over the past decades, and more specifically so in developing economies. However, there is a major divide in the types of loan products and purpose of borrowing between advanced and developing economies. While in advanced economies residential mortgages have long been the dominant type of household credit, in developing economies consumer credit, credit card loans, and car loans make up most household credit, and mortgage lending has stagnated as a percentage of total household credit. While some consumer lending is likely used for home improvements and expansions, estimates of the volume of microfinance for housing show the small size of this sector, particularly in sub-Saharan Africa.

Demographic and economic trends

Demand opportunities

Recent changes in the housing finance sector have taken place in an environment of stabilizing economic growth and decreasing poverty levels in most developing countries. Overall economic growth in low- and middle-income countries was 4.5 per cent for 2018, ranging from highs of 6.9 per cent in South Asia to ~3 per cent in sub-Saharan Africa and the Middle East, with Latin America being an outlier at 1.7 per cent.[12] These figures are well above population growth figures in most countries and bode well for improvements in household incomes. Indeed, low- and middle-income countries have seen a steady increase in the middle-income segment of the population. Increasing income levels are, other things being equal, correlated with growth in housing demand, i.e. the willingness to pay a certain proportion of income for housing.

Equally important is the fact that the world has experienced a dramatic fall in absolute poverty in the last 30 years or so. In 1990, more than one-third of the world's population was below the absolute poverty line; by 2015, it was 10 per cent and falling. This extraordinarily rapid rise in the economic well-being of the world's poorest is without historical precedent (World Bank, 2018b). In absolute terms, these figures show that the largest number of the world's poor now live in large middle-income countries (which include China, India, Pakistan, Bangladesh, Indonesia, and others).

There is an important qualifier, however. The poverty-line methodology measures poverty levels only in monetary terms. If non-monetary indicators of poverty are included in the global measure of poverty – and these include access to water, sanitation, and electricity – the poverty or deprivation figures increase dramatically. Approximately 25 per cent of the population in the 119 countries included in the World Bank survey live in houses that lack access to even limited standards of sanitation. Even regions with low monetary poverty such as East Asia and the Pacific, Latin America and the Caribbean, the Middle East, and North Africa, suffer a sanitation deprivation rate several times as high as the monetary poverty measure alone.

According to a recent World Bank report on poverty in East Asia and the Pacific, poor quality housing as an indicator of non-monetary poverty affects 75 per cent of the extreme poor, as perhaps expected, but also a full quarter of the *economically secure* population in selected countries (World Bank, 2018c: 71). These figures are considerably higher in other regions of the developing world, and are consistent with the observations of the lagging investments in urban housing and residential infrastructure relative to GDP discussed below.[13] Importantly, poor housing conditions in urban areas of the developing world affect renters disproportionally. According to recent estimates, 70 to 80 per cent of households in cities of sub-Saharan Africa are renters, living mostly in private, informal room-rentals of various types, a figure that has increased during the past few decades.[14] While the proportion of renter households is somewhat lower in Latin American and Asian cities, it is important to realize that the private rental sector is a significant provider of affordable urban housing (UN Habitat & Cities Alliance, 2011). Thus, strategies to deal with housing and housing finance for the world's underserved populations need to be based on an inclusive definition of underserved groups: poor and not so poor, informally and formally employed, renters and owners, and those with different types of tenure, types of collateral, and property rights.

Demand challenges

Scaling up housing and housing finance solutions for the underserved poses enormous challenges, particularly in large urban areas of rapidly urbanizing countries in Asia and Africa, where formal housing construction has lagged well behind population and household growth. Urbanization alone will add some 2 billion new urbanites in those regions in the next two decades. For example, India, which is expected to be the most populous country in the world, will see its urban population increase from 33 per cent to 52 per cent by 2050. Many sub-Saharan countries will increase their urban populations at a similar rate.[15] Yet formal housing production for the low- and middle-income segments is severely constrained because of the growing mismatch between house prices and incomes, the small size and high interest costs of housing finance systems, and inefficiencies in land and development markets.

The challenges to address the urban housing needs of rapidly growing urban areas in developing countries have become more intractable in recent decades since urbanization happens at income levels lower than during the rapid urban growth of earlier periods (Glaeser, 2014). Low urban incomes, and the related small tax base, hamper public investment in housing and residential infrastructure. A study by the World Bank confirms that urban housing investment, by public and private sectors and including both formal and informal structures, has not kept pace with urbanization in low- and lower-middle income countries (Dasgupta et al., 2014). As a consequence, the increase of urban informal housing developments and slum formation has continued (even if at a slower pace than in previous decades), which puts a heavy burden on infrastructure, transport systems, and the environment, and comes with high human and social costs.

In the middle-income countries of Latin America, house construction, aided by large-scale government housing finance programmes (see Box 1.2), is roughly keeping up with urban population increase but the proportion of households in inadequate housing is still very large. Concerns have shifted mostly to upgrading existing substandard housing, a legacy of the region's fast urban growth period.

In addition, many low-income housing areas are affected by growing environmental risks, due to the combined forces of increased housing developments in areas subject to flooding and other natural risks and climate change impacts. Countries of East and South Asia (China, India, Pakistan, Indonesia, the Philippines, Vietnam) are particularly prone to hydrological disasters (Guha-Sapir et al., 2016). Changing storm and precipitation patterns and sea-level rise will require massive resettlements and reinforcement of existing houses to make them disaster resistant, adding to the overall requirements for housing and housing finance for the lower-income segments.

These demographic and environmental trends, and the mismatch between demand and supply of adequate housing in low- and lower-middle income countries, come at a high economic and societal cost, including:

1. *The human cost of having over a billion urban dwellers living in inadequate housing in places that lack access to basic infrastructure* (transportation, electricity, water, sanitation), urban services (education, health) and public spaces (space for parks and community facilities such as schools, health

---

Box 1.2 The subsidy debate

In an effort to make housing affordable in growing urban areas, several countries implemented housing programmes for ownership that offered subsidized credit and/ or down-payment support to low- and middle-income households. These subsidy programmes defined maximum house prices affordable for different income segments. House construction was done mostly by private developers who did not take market risk, allowing them to go to scale. However, they would build mostly on cheap land beyond the periphery of cities where large-scale, green-field sites were available. While subsidies unlocked the building of many units, the location of housing projects in faraway locations without adequate transport and services made it impossible for low-income households to reach employment, schools, and other services within a reasonable amount of time and without incurring extremely high transportation costs. As a consequence, many households would leave these homes and stop paying their loans, which resulted in high levels of non-performing loans and widespread vacancies (Monkkonen, 2018).

The housing commission in Mexico overhauled its subsidized housing programme in 2011 after experiencing extremely high vacancy rates and related delinquency (OECD, 2015; Monkkonen, 2014). Location criteria were introduced, restricting the subsidy programme to properties within a certain distance from the centre. The eligible area was subsequently divided into three zones according to job density and access to water and sanitation, defined yearly by the government. The level of subsidy varied by location: more central locations received higher subsidies to compensate for higher land costs (Acolin et al., 2019).

The poor outcomes of finance-linked housing subsidy programmes in some emerging market countries, including Mexico, Chile, and Brazil, have fuelled a negative attitude towards housing finance for lower-income households. However, the problem was not the provision of housing credit, but rather the stress on household budgets of additional transportation costs, the low quality of life in poorly serviced remote areas, and most of all the related low resale value of the property relative to the loan amount (Acolin et al., 2019).[16] While, like in Mexico, many of these programmes have since been redesigned, access to housing finance and related subsidies remain necessary components of these programmes.

These experiences show that housing finance and credit-linked housing programmes, meant to extend formal home-ownership to the lowest income groups, cannot be viewed in isolation from factors such as labour, housing, land markets, and social networks. Households have preferences that must be respected if such programmes are to succeed.

---

care centres), or are at high risk of flooding or other natural disasters. And this number is predicted to more than double in the next 30 years, with high human costs and cost to the environment (United Nations, 2014).

2. *High cost of fragmented and informal housing developments and poorly planned cities to the wider economy and to city dwellers.* While cities are generally engines of economic growth because of various agglomeration effects, this benefit is often not realized when most housing supply is informal and not linked to the necessary infrastructure. Traffic congestion and high cost of service delivery make many cities extremely inefficient with negative effects on housing costs for its citizens and on overall economic growth (Lall et al., 2017).[17]

3. *Constraints on the development of housing finance systems.* Low incomes relative to housing costs, high levels of informal employment, and a lack of property rights and registration systems make the development

of a formal housing finance system difficult, whether mortgage or non-mortgage based. Without access to finance, housing construction by the public or private sector, whether for ownership or renting, will remain limited to those market segments for which the formal mortgage market works or cash transactions are common (Hoek-Smit et al., 2018).

4. *Worsening economic inequality.* The reliance on informal housing, mostly without title or ownership rights, and informal renting as the main housing solution for lower and lower-middle-income households, limits the accumulation of housing assets (or wealth) by a large part of the population. This worsens economic or wealth inequality in countries where income inequality is already an issue of growing concern (World Inequality Lab, 2018).

Towards an integrated housing finance system

The small size of the combined mortgage and housing microfinance sectors in low- and middle-income countries is cause for concern, given the enormous requirement for new housing and housing improvement. Rather than fearing the expansion of housing finance systems appropriate for the different underserved segments of the population, as in the 'financialization' debates (Box 1.1), new ways have to be found to speed up the expansion of housing finance for the underserved, to help improve their housing situation whether through gradual home improvement, incremental loans, or mortgage loans for finished new or existing houses. Without a vibrant and diverse housing finance sector, the positive social and economic features of the housing sector cannot be unlocked. A holistic view of the housing finance sector for the underserved has to guide the reform agenda both through government policy and private sector innovations in order to expand access to housing finance in a safe and sustainable way that will not expose households or lenders to undue risks.

Scaling up microfinance for housing

The size of microfinance for housing and micro-mortgage lending is still extremely small relative to the growing demand for housing credit. The focus for the development of the sector needs to broaden beyond access and inclusion and pay more attention to scalability and efficiency of solutions. Several studies have shown that smaller loan sizes and outreach efforts have a negative effect on interest rates and overall profitability of the financial institution.[18] How can the sector scale up while improving its performance? Measures such as levels of interest rates and lending margins, levels of non-performing loans, and overall profitability of microfinance for housing institutions are key for expansion.

The many new ways that have been developed to achieve those outcomes will be discussed in Chapters 2, 3, 4, and 5. These include: reduced transaction costs, including through the use of fintech applications; reduced credit risk through the general use of credit bureaus and other innovative data systems; improved governance systems and institutional structures of small microfinance institutions; a growing number of investors to expand the funding base of housing finance for the world's poor; a diverse range of housing finance products for both ownership and rental housing, which suits the requirements of different households and housing preferences and builds on principles of consumer protection; and entry of new players and improved regulation. One major unresolved area is the tension between increasing the productivity and profitability of housing microfinance institutions and the outreach and support efforts to poor customers needed to ensure construction quality, which is critical for success as shown in Chapters 3 and 4.

Such comprehensive development of housing microfinance requires considerable capacity development in both the private and public sectors.

Deepening mortgage markets for the underserved

Equally, the stagnation in the growth of mortgage markets in developing countries needs to be addressed urgently in order for formal housing markets to expand to creditworthy lower-income households and informally employed. Mortgage loans are larger, have a longer term, are cheaper, and facilitate, therefore, access to formal housing for the large underserved lower-middle-income segment in many countries.

What structural problems hinder expansion? The core structural factors include macro-economic volatility, which hinders longer-term lending particularly; impaired or utterly incomplete property rights and registration systems as discussed in Chapter 2; and monopolies in the housing finance sector of mostly public mortgage finance institutions.[19] In the meantime, the mortgage industry in many countries is developing new technologies and creating new systems and procedures to reduce transaction costs, deal with default and collateral risks, and manage interest rate risks through various capital market instruments, as discussed in Chapter 5. The unprecedented technological developments and the use of alternative underwriting data make it possible to provide mortgage loans to informally employed but creditworthy clients and to open up the market of existing affordable houses in formal but low-income neighbourhoods. These innovations considerably expand the mortgage frontier in many countries. Studies show that if government policies focus on the structural issues of the industry, such as the property registration system and improved competition, the industry will develop the tools to improve overall efficiency and risk management systems (Mengistu and Perez-Saiz, 2018).[20]

Market integration to improve mobility

Lastly, a holistic policy strategy needs to facilitate the interconnectedness between the two housing finance sectors and create a flexible housing finance market for the diverse underserved population. Income and poverty data show that households improve their economic status over time, but that housing poverty and inequality remain major issues. Moreover, urban labour markets have changed and require workers to move more frequently to new employment opportunities. Creating options for housing mobility should guide policy just as much as goals to expand access or inclusion. But what constrains housing mobility for those who value and can afford homeownership? The lack of affordable existing or new housing is of course a major hindrance. However, the housing finance system could assist poor households to gradually improve their current home through a sequence of microfinance loans as discussed in Chapter 3 and, while doing so, build up not just the value of their home but a credit record that allows them to eventually acquire a regular mortgage loan to pay for an existing house in a better neighbourhood, for example. Finance to construct affordable rental units by private landlords, often in the form of added units to an owner-occupied house where the rental income secures loan repayment, also improves options for housing mobility.

Access to a sequence of different housing finance products will require first of all that appropriate products are offered by a diverse and large number of financial institutions including coops, credit unions, and non-bank financial institutions, which share client credit profiles across the industry (Agarwal et al., 2018).[21] In other words, much greater mobility and housing affordability can be achieved in currently very restrictive formal markets when mortgage lenders have the tools to include existing (and often cheaper) housing in their lending portfolio, and the microfinance sector diversifies their loan products, professionalizes, and is included in a well-functioning credit information system. Policy-makers, regulators, industry leaders, and investors all have a critical role to play in this market development and integration. The chapters of this book are meant to provide guidance to this process through state-of-the-art reviews and case studies.

Conclusion

Since the publication of the two books that are the reference point for the current volume on housing finance for the large underserved population – Daphnis and Ferguson's *Housing Microfinance* in 2004 and Prahalad's *The Fortune at the Bottom of the Pyramid* in 2006 – major disruptions as well as positive changes in the global housing finance landscape have occurred that make revisiting this critical area important and necessary (Daphnis and Ferguson, 2004 and Prahalad, 2006).

The authors of both books were inspired by a similar urge to change the perspective of society and, particularly, of the private sector, to demonstrate the business opportunities in catering to consumer needs in underserved markets for housing and other goods and services. Both emphasized that lending to the poor can be profitable and that regulations which force banks to serve a certain underserved group will not be needed once this potential is better understood. At that time, housing microfinance was still in its infancy. Risks were considered high since housing is not necessarily income producing, and, therefore, does not assist households' repayment capacity. And unlike mortgage credit, housing microfinance does not allow lenders access to the housing asset in case of non-payment.

Now, 15 years later, a much deeper understanding exists of the complementary roles of government policy and the private sector, and of the range of products and institutions needed to make housing finance available to different segments of the underserved market, both for ownership and rental housing. This came about in part through lessons learned from crises including the microfinance crisis in the Indian state of Andhra Pradesh, the Mexican housing crisis, the global financial crisis, and beyond. But also through powerful examples of thriving and sophisticated housing finance institutions that specialize in delivering diverse housing finance services to hitherto excluded customers. A shift has occurred, particularly in developing economies, away from a focus on microfinance per se to a concern for financial inclusion, scaling, and sustainability of housing finance for the underserved, supported by new technologies such as mobile phones, alternative sources of data, and new funding mechanisms. The housing finance sector, with its high requirements for information on the housing asset as well as on households' ability and willingness to pay for a housing loan, is expanding its credit offerings in this new environment.

Indeed, the range of players in the housing finance arena that focus on the underserved has expanded enormously and includes not just microfinance institutions but mainstream banks, non-bank housing finance companies, e-commerce institutions, debt and equity funds, fintech companies, insurance companies, and more. It is therefore an excellent time to look at new developments in housing finance and understand both the opportunities and the challenges that exist on the demand and supply side of the housing and the housing finance market for the underserved segment.

Notes

1. Private credit in OECD countries. The Organisation for Economic Co-operation and Development is made up of 36 mostly high-income countries that reached 100 per cent of GDP in the late 2000s, compared to around 30 per cent in the 1950s. In developing economies the ratio has remained stable over the past decades at 40 per cent to 45 per cent of GDP. While this is still a substantial private credit growth in real terms, it is interesting to understand the different drivers behind private sector credit between advanced and emerging market countries since it is directly relevant for our understanding of housing finance for the underserved.

2. A harmonized new data set including 120 countries with data from >600 intermediaries including non-bank financial institutions. 'Credit is defined to include all debt contracts (loans and debt securities) denominated in

local or foreign currency'. Countries typically report time series on loans extended by all monetary financial institutions. These data are, therefore, close to *bank credit* data reported by WB Global Financial Data Base, which is relevant for this study, rather than *total debt* data (IMF data base).

3. Construction and real estate loans have increased as a percentage of the aggregate corporate loan portfolio since the 1990s both in OECD countries and developing economies and went up from 5 per cent in the 1950s to almost 20 per cent in 2018.

4. The data does not reveal the actual proportion of mortgage loans in advanced economies that was used for housing acquisition or improvements. Mortgage refinancing loans, which are often 40 per cent to 50 per cent of all mortgage loans in the US and other advanced economies, were often used to take out accumulated equity in the property to pay for education and consumption, certainly in the period of easy credit allocation during the run up to the global financial crisis.

5. These figures do not include instalment loans by developers, which are an important source of housing finance when mortgages are expensive or difficult to obtain. Instalment loan portfolios can be larger than mortgage loan portfolios in some countries in the Middle East and Africa. Such loans are used mostly by middle-income households and are not regulated in most countries, exposing the buyer to high risks.

6. 111 countries included; Mortgage debt to GDP defined by total amount of home mortgage loans outstanding at the end of year as % of GDP (current); Low to High income categories based on 2017 World Bank classifications; Very high income where GNI per capita > $30,000 (Atlas method, 2017).

7. Habitat for Humanity estimate. Lecture Notes. IHFP, Wharton 2019.

8. See, for example, Muller, 2018; and Hofinet.org

9. However, microfinance institutions often require some proof of ownership of the property, even if there is no official lien involved, and are therefore similarly hampered by the lack of property rights systems.

10. See, for example: Leilani Farha, Special Rapporteur on the right to adequate housing (2017) United Nations Human Rights Council, UN Habitat.

11. Studies have shown that mortgage credit growth in the run up to the crisis and driven in part by the availability of structured finance mechanisms, was not a low-income or subprime borrower phenomenon but shared across income groups and across prime and subprime mortgages. When the bubble burst and house prices came down, *many more homes were lost by prime mortgage borrowers not just early in the crisis but for several years after the crisis.*

12. IMF. Data Mapper. Projections for 2019 are lower, but a rebound is projected for 2020 and beyond.

13. In particular in countries of sub-Saharan Africa and part of North Africa.

14. South Africa is an exception with urban rental figures in the order of 50 per cent because of its massive low-income home-ownership programme.

15. UN and World Bank data (2018).

16. Acolin et al. (2019) find that default rates under the MCMV programme in Brazil for the lowest income bracket are significantly higher in peripheral areas.

17. City dwellers in the cities included in their study paid 55 per cent more for housing, 35 per cent more for food, and 42 per cent more for transport than city dwellers in a sample of other low- and middle-income countries.

18. The study included data from 292 MFIs in 34 countries of sub-Saharan Africa from 2003–2011: Habitat for Humanity, 2017, ibid.
19. New technologies to map properties and create registration systems have opened possibilities to address this major constraint for mortgage market expansion. The next step is to create the legal framework for these alternative technologies to be codified. Zambia is one of the first countries in sub-Saharan Africa to have done so recently.
20. The data show that competition tends to increase the probability of access to several finance products, particularly credit, more than bank balance sheet variables such as capital adequacy or liquidity.
21. The paper shows the case of a large microcredit expansion programme in Rwanda serving previously unbanked persons. A sizable proportion of these first-time borrowers switch to larger and cheaper bank loans for their second loans.

References

Acolin, A., Hoek-Smit, M. and Magelean, C. (2019) 'High delinquency rates in Brazil's Minha Casa Minha Vida housing program: possible causes and necessary reforms', *Habitat International* 83: 99–110.

Agarwal, S., Kigabo, T., Minoiu, C., Presbitero, A. and Silva, A. (2018) *Financial Inclusion under the Microscope*, IMF Working Paper 18/208, International Monetary Fund, Washington, DC.

Albanesi S., De Giorgi G. and Nosal J. (August 2017) 'Credit Growth and the Financial Crisis: A New Narrative' *NBER Working Paper* No. 23740

Daphnis, F. and Ferguson, B. (2004) *Housing Microfinance: A Guide to Practice*, Kumarian Press Inc., Bloomfield, CT.

Dasgupta, B., Lall, S.V. and Lazano-Gracia, N. (2014) *Urbanization and Housing Investment*, World Bank Policy Paper 7110, World Bank, Washington, DC.

De Jager, P. (2016) *Housing Microfinance Business Models: Three Cases* CAHF; Chikalipah, Sydney (2018) 'Why are Microcredit Interest Rates in sub-Saharan Africa so Persistently High? Testing the Predictions of Theoretical Models', *PhD thesis for Cape Town University.*

Ferreira, F. (2018) 'Mortgage Lending and Housing Markets' *NBER Reporter* Number 3.

Ferreira, F. and Gyourko J., June 2015 'A New Look at the U.S. Foreclosure Crisis: Panel Data Evidence of Prime and Subprime Borrowers from 1997 to 2012' *NBER Working Paper* No. 21261.

Glaeser, E. (2014) 'A world of cities: the causes and consequences of urbanization in poorer countries', *Journal of the European Economic Association* 12(5): 1154–99 <https://doi.org/10.1111/jeea.12100>.

Guha-Sapir, D., Hoyois, P., Wallemacq, P. and Below, R. (2016) *Annual Disaster Statistical Review 2016: The Numbers and Trends*, CRED, Brussels.

Habitat for Humanity (2017) *The 2016–2017 State of Housing Microfinance: Understanding the Business Case for Housing Microfinance*, Terwilliger Center for Innovation in Shelter, Habitat for Humanity, Atlanta, GA.

Hoek-Smit, M.C., Kim, K.H. and Wachter, S. (2018) *Cities and Affordable Housing: Fulfilling the New Urban Agenda*, Working Paper no. 829, Samuel Zell & Robert Lurie Real Estate Center, Wharton School, University of Pennsylvania, Philadelphia.

Lall, S.V., Vernon Henderson, J. and Venerables, A. (2017) *Africa's Cities: Opening the Doors to the World*, World Bank, Washington, DC.

Mengistu, A. and Perez-Saiz, H. (2018) *Financial Inclusion and Bank Competition in Sub-Saharan Africa*, IMF Working Paper 18/256, International Monetary Fund, Washington, DC.

Monkkonen, P. (2014) *The Role of Housing Finance in Mexico's Vacancy Crisis*, Working Paper, UCLA Ziman Center for Real Estate, University of California, Los Angeles.

Monkkonen, P. (2018) 'Empty houses across North America: housing finance and Mexico's vacancy crisis', *Urban Studies* 56(10): 2075–91 <https://doi.org/10.1177/0042098018788024>.

Müller, K. (2018) *Credit Markets Around the World, 1910–2014*, SSRN <http://dx.doi.org/10.2139/ssrn.3259636>.

OECD (2015) *OECD Urban Policy Reviews: Mexico 2015: Transforming Urban Policy and Housing Finance*, OECD Publishing, Paris <https://doi.org/10.1787/9789264227293-en>.

Prahalad, C.K. (2006) *The Fortune at the Bottom of the Pyramid*, Wharton School Publishing, Saddle River, NJ.

Schularick, M. and Taylor (2012) 'A. M. Credit booms gone bust: Monetary policy, leverage cycles, and financial crises, 1870–2008' *American Economic Review* 102(2): 1029–1061.

UN Habitat & Cities Alliance (2011) *Housing the Poor in African Cities: Quick Guide 7: Rental Housing: a much neglected housing option for the poor*, United Nations Human Settlements Programme (UN HABITAT), Nairobi.

World Bank (2018a) *2017 Global Findex Survey* <https://globalfindex.worldbank.org>.

World Bank (2018b) *Poverty and Shared Prosperity 2018: Piecing Together the Poverty Puzzle*, World Bank, Washington, DC.

World Bank (2018c) *Riding the Wave, An East Asian Miracle for the 21st Century*, World Bank East and Pacific Regional Report, World Bank, Washington, DC.

World Inequality Lab (2018) *World Inequality Report 2018*, World Inequality Lab, Paris.

Author biography

Drs. Marja Hoek-Smit is founder and director of the International Housing Finance Programme, Wharton School, University of Pennsylvania. She is a frequent advisor to governments and private- and non-profit sector clients in emerging markets and developing countries in the field of housing and housing finance policy, and the executive director of the Housing Finance Information Network (HOFINET), a global web portal that consolidates international housing finance information and statistical data for public use.

CHAPTER 2

The housing finance ecosystem for the world's poor

Daniel Rozas and Patrick McAllister

The housing finance ecosystem is defined by the laws, practices, and institutions that govern land ownership, building codes, and finance. Within finance alone, the ecosystem consists of multiple layers including regulatory rules and infrastructure, a variety of types and sources of investment and funding, and institutions, products, and services provided to clients. This ecosystem functions alongside a deep and well-developed informal finance market that plays a major role in most developing countries. The chapter closes with a deep dive into the ecosystem in India, providing a view to how these many components interact in practice.

Keywords: housing finance; financial regulation; land policy; building codes; construction practices; housing microfinance; micro-mortgage; India

> There are these two young fish swimming along, and they happen to meet an older fish swimming the other way, who nods at them and says, 'Morning, boys, how's the water?' And the two young fish swim on for a bit, and then eventually one of them looks over at the other and goes, 'What the hell is water?'
> —David Foster Wallace

The housing ecosystem is the 'water' within which housing microfinance operates. Like the young fish, most people are unaware of the network of institutions, regulations, products, and services that work together to ensure they can access the materials, financing, and technical help they need to build and improve their homes. Nor is there any need for them to have such awareness. The system that determines the options they have for home improvement operates in the background. Any actor within that system – from homeowner, to bank CEO, to minister of housing – interacts with just a portion of the many components that comprise the ecosystem.

Housing is one of the most complex segments of the economy, with a multitude of interdependent parts, each of which has an impact on the housing options for over a billion poor people. Of course, not all of the people living in substandard housing are buying, building, or improving homes. Many rent and some have no home at all, forced to sleep where

http://dx.doi.org/10.3362/9781730447681.003

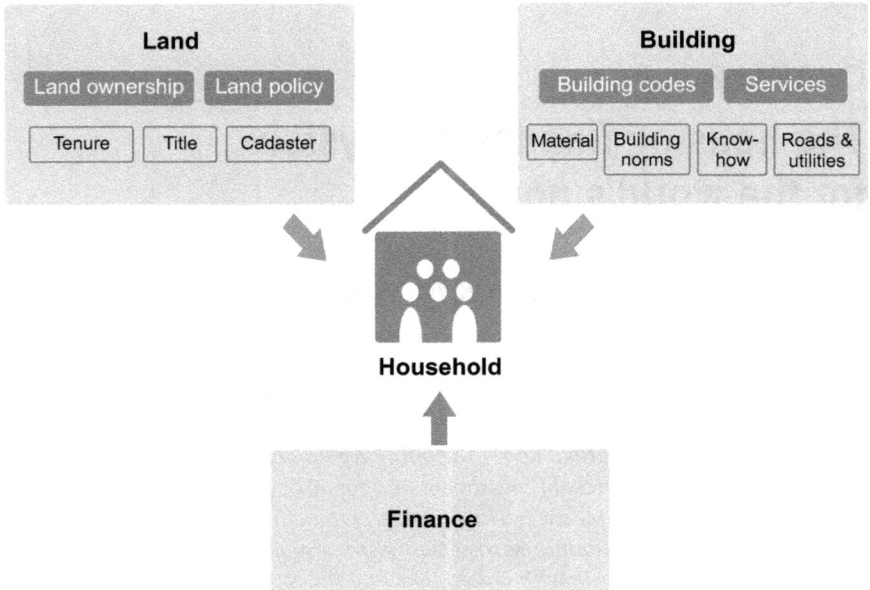

Figure 2.1 The housing ecosystem

they can. The financing options discussed in this book, like housing microfinance and micro-mortgages, cannot solve all housing needs. Building more affordable rental units and developing an appropriate level of social housing provided by the state are important objectives, but they are outside the scope of this book.

For those who build or buy affordable homes, the ecosystem can be divided into four major components as illustrated in Figure 2.1: the households themselves, land, building, and finance. While this book is focused on finance, it is important to briefly describe the other components so that the role of finance can be properly understood.

Households

At the centre of the ecosystem are the households themselves, because the ecosystem exists to provide people with places to live. Yet not all households are equal in this ecosystem. Far too often the needs of poor families get little attention from builders, funders, and policy-makers, whose decisions and practices are at best guided by the needs of the wealthy, and at worst driven by corruption and dishonesty. That's not the case in this book, where poor families like those whose stories are told in Chapter 3 are at the centre, and everything else is organized around them.

The International Finance Corporation (IFC) estimates that 1.2 billon people lack adequate housing, and this is expected to increase to 3 billion by

2030, a trend set by growing urbanization which itself is slated to increase city populations by 2.5 billion people by 2050 (United Nations, 2018 & World Bank, 2016).[1] Most of that additional urban population will be concentrated in Africa and Asia. In their pioneering report, *A Blueprint for Addressing the Global Affordable Housing Challenge*, the McKinsey Global Institute estimated that USD 10 *trillion* would be needed to improve the living conditions for all those living in substandard housing by 2025, not including the cost of land (McKinsey, 2014). This figure includes substandard housing in both industrialized and developing economies, but the demand is much higher in the latter.[2]

In fact, the problem is likely greater than the McKinsey data indicates. That study was focused on cities, but in countries that are predominantly poor and rural (such as India) substandard housing in rural areas is as high or higher than in cities. For the foreseeable future, quality housing will continue to be in very high demand in both urban and rural areas across the developing world.

Land

No housing can be built without land; it is the foundation on which everything else rests. Factors that affect access to land comprise the first leg of the housing ecosystem. Types of land ownership vary greatly between different countries, ranging from individual freehold ownership to communal rights and temporal leasehold on government-owned land. Land law and policy, including aspects of zoning and land use planning, guide how land may be used and what types of structures may be built on it.

Incremental building happens everywhere, under all types of land ownership and land policies; often informally without government-issued permits or clearly documented land rights. Even so, secure, well-defined ownership plays an important role in facilitating housing finance. For mortgage finance, including micro-mortgages, clear ownership with a title to the property is explicitly required.[3] For housing microfinance, evidence of property rights can be more flexible, but rarely do financial institutions approve loans for housing without some evidence of land rights.[4] Understanding the types of land rights in a given market is critical for any actor involved in housing finance.

The laws, practices, and infrastructure that govern land ownership (collectively known as tenure, title, and cadaster) form the building blocks of property rights. They define: the types of rights recognized; how parcel boundaries are recorded and demarcated; the rights, restrictions, and responsibilities inherent in a particular property; and how land transactions are to be recorded. Where these mechanisms and the broader government land

administration system function efficiently, they prevent uncertainty and conflict over land and allow for the creation of an asset.

The cadaster is a record of the boundaries of different parcels of land. Unfortunately, many countries don't have well-functioning cadastral systems, and those that do often cover only limited areas. The cadaster doesn't prove ownership or land rights, however. For that, a title or deed is needed – the official, government-issued document, usually registered with a state body, that provides the highest level of proof that a specific piece of land belongs to a certain individual. Because of this, title can be used as collateral for borrowing. This level of title (often called hard title) can be difficult or expensive for poor households to obtain. Various lesser forms of documentation are often used to prove ownership rights in practice. Some examples of these alternative forms of title include locally (as opposed to nationally) registered documents – such as an occupancy certificate, receipts for property tax payment, or an entry in a village ledger. Chapter 4 provides real world examples of alternative titles accepted by certain financial institutions.

Property boundaries and proof of ownership may also be informal, dependent on agreements within the local community and its leadership. Indeed, individual ownership is not always possible. Some land is governed by shared tribal or communal ownership rules. In all cases, the body of laws, regulations, and customs that govern land boundaries and ownership determine use, and greatly influence the type of housing finance available.

Ownership can also be dynamic. Even where the occupant is clearly not the owner of land, building a more permanent structure can sometimes be a reasonable path to secure ownership, with the occupied land eventually becoming formalized in favour of the occupant. Many illegal slums that started as squatter settlements have, over time, been formalized into city neighbourhoods complete with utilities, transport, and other government services, alongside formal recognition of ownership by the erstwhile squatters.

For many of the world's poor, land administration – a foundational layer of the housing ecosystem — is failing. The result of this failure is urban slums, built on land with no formal demarcation, no system to prove ownership, and no enforcement of encroachment on land held by others. Lack of land administration has resulted in housing for the poor built in unsafe and inappropriate locations such as flood zones, steep slopes, or ecologically sensitive areas. Millions of households live in such circumstances, with little or none of the infrastructure necessary for decent housing, such as roads, water, sanitation, and energy. Informality also increases the risk of eviction without recourse.

Between those at this extreme and those with fully formalized property, there are many gradations of tenure that allow housing microfinance providers to finance the construction or improvement of their homes.

Building

The second leg of the ecosystem consists of factors that affect the physical structure itself. As with land, government policies can play a major role in housing construction. The basic premise of establishing building codes is to assure safety and city planning.

Building

Building codes		Services	
Material	Building norms	Know-how	Roads & utilities

But building codes are generally designed for commercial buildings or formal housing of the upper-middle classes and above. For the world's poor they are often overly restrictive and inflexible, and open to corruption where building approval depends more on the size of a bribe than on a well-designed building plan. It should not be surprising that most of the households presented in Chapter 3 did not build their homes to any sort of code, and their homes are exposed to greater risk as a result. A more flexible and realistic system of building codes would ensure that quality housing is available for families of all financial means.

Services are another key element of quality housing: roads, water, sewerage, electricity, trash collection, and (the most recent additions to housing adequacy) mobile and digital connections. Many poor communities around the world, whether urban slums or rural villages, are defined by the absence of these services. The result is a sad mix of washed out roads and weak transportation links, poor sanitation due to scarcity of affordable clean water, and darkness – both digital and electric. Indeed, one of the easiest ways to identify poverty is simply to look at night-time satellite imagery; the poor cast little light compared to their wealthy counterparts.

Inadequate services are the fruits of poor government planning and loose stewardship of scarce resources, exacerbated by their unequal allocation and outright corruption. The high pace of urbanization creates additional challenges that restrict services in poorly funded municipalities. In the absence of such services, the poor find their own solutions. Some common examples include installing rooftop solar panels for electricity instead of accessing the grid, digging wells instead of connecting to water mains, and installing septic tanks or simply channelling waste to the street instead of connecting to sewerage.

Building *practices* also affect construction and the role it plays in affordable housing. Local practices differ, guided by the type and affordability of construction materials available, as well as local knowledge and tradition. Perhaps surprisingly, poor families around the world, especially in southern climates, typically aspire to homes that follow a remarkably similar pattern: walls built with concrete blocks or reinforced cement, and roofing consisting of corrugated metal sheets. To a large degree this is the result of the ubiquitous availability and easy transportability of these materials, produced on a massive scale globally and available in local hardware stores or cement depots. Due to the perceived permanence of these materials, they can sometimes be seen as

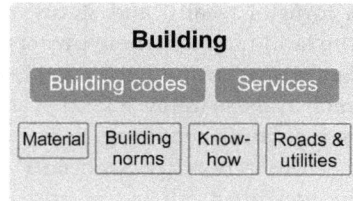

a form of wealth and status, and a means to stake a more secure claim to the land in cases where ownership is otherwise uncertain. Similar houses dot landscapes around the world, irrespective of country or continent. Homes such as these follow a kind of standardization even when there is no authority or regulation requiring it.

Ironically, this 'standard' home is preferred even when local alternatives are both better and less costly. For example, in many countries bamboo is an abundantly available and inexpensive local material that is also flexible against earthquakes. Roofing constructed from natural fibres is more effective at cooling and safer in the face of high winds (unlike metal sheeting, which strong hurricanes can turn into veritable missiles). Natural, locally sourced materials are often less costly, but they are viewed as 'old-fashioned' by poor households and considered temporary at best, until the household can afford more modern materials. Design and marketing of durable and environmentally sustainable materials can be made attractive and aspirational to poor households that build their homes incrementally, but doing so requires changing attitudes and expectations.

Finance

The last leg in the housing ecosystem is finance. It is neither the most important nor the most complex element in the ecosystem, but it is the topic of this book and hence will be discussed in more detail than the other

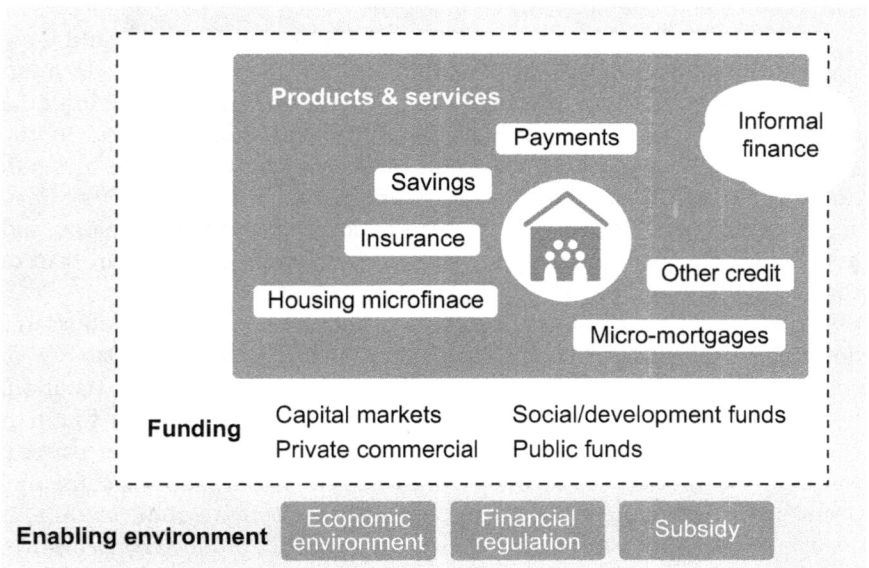

Figure 2.2 The housing finance ecosystem

elements. The purpose here is to provide a framework that helps demonstrate how each component fits within the broader picture and how they interact with each other. Subsequent chapters will cover many of the components in greater detail.

Access to housing finance by the billion-plus households living in inadequate housing can be understood through three key factors: 1) the total available income that can be devoted to housing; 2) the sources and composition of that income, including degree of formality and earners in the household; and 3) possession of, or ability to secure, a formal title. These three factors largely define the finance options available to these households. Top earners (making up less than 5 per cent of the population in most developing countries) are the least likely to be living in inadequate housing and are the only ones that can access traditional mortgage finance. They have relatively high incomes that are well documented and received from formal sources. They also have, or can secure, a formal title to the property they want to build, improve, or buy. Much effort is invested in deepening and improving the functioning of mortgage markets that serve these middle- and upper-income groups.[5] Even so, the challenges of expanding long-term finance in many markets mean that even those with sufficient income can find it difficult to secure a long-term mortgage loan.

However, the focus of this book is on those who are not, or at least not yet, in the middle class. Two of the factors described above play a critical role in limiting access to traditional housing finance for these populations: lack of formal property title and reliance on informal incomes. Innovations in the ability of financial institutions to provide poor households with housing finance, even given these factors, have jump-started the inclusive housing finance sector.

Products & services

Micro-mortgages

For those in the upper reaches of the poor – not quite middle class but with sufficient (though often informal) household incomes to repay a substantial loan – one recent innovation has been the development of micro-mortgages. These loans require a fully documented property title as collateral and thus often satisfy regulatory requirements for secured loans. This designation allows financial institutions to avail of refinance, lower capital requirements, and other benefits of secured lending. Micro-mortgage loans feature smaller amounts and often shorter terms than a traditional mortgage, making them attractive for the smaller homes required by low-income households. But what distinguishes them most from traditional mortgages is that they can accommodate informal incomes and income from extended families. In India, where there has been a growth in small, low-cost apartments in multi-unit complexes in or just outside urban areas, micro-mortgages have become an affordable solution for low-income earners.

Housing microfinance

For households that do not possess the formal title required by a mortgage or micro-mortgage loan, inclusive housing finance offers another innovation: the housing microfinance loan. Based on well-established microfinance practice, this product allows households to tap meaningful credit for incremental building, improvement, or renovation. Using proven practices of finance for poor households, housing microfinance is well adapted to the self-building practices presented in Chapter 3, where home building has been accelerated using microfinance loans. It works particularly well for incremental building in rural and low- to medium-density urban areas, but is less suited to building a home all at once or for purchasing an already built home. Housing microfinance can also finance investment in basic services like water, sanitation, and energy, which improve the quality of the home (see Box 2.1 in this chapter and the case of Nikhil in Chapter 3). Chapter 4 delves deeply into the practices behind housing microfinance.

Other credit

Those with few financial options will necessarily make use of whatever funding is available, and studies show that around 20 per cent of the proceeds of loans intended for investment in micro-enterprise are redirected to housing (Daphnis and Ferguson, 2004: 23). Two such borrowers (Nisrine and Panna) are presented in Chapter 3. However, the practice of diverting a business loan to housing is sub-optimal. Microfinance loans for working capital are typically shorter term and have lower amounts than required for home improvement. This practice also presents a false picture of loan use to the lender, so that risk management and planning is more likely to miss important trends or exposures that should be monitored.

Remittances

Housing finance is not limited to credit, of course. Among poor households in developing countries a critical source of funding for housing is remittances sent by spouses, adult children, or other household members working away from home, whether elsewhere in the country or abroad. This will be seen in detail in the following chapter, where Panna's income depended almost entirely on remittances from her husband working in Singapore and sent via the *hawala* system. Their arrival didn't always match the timing of housing expenses. As a result, she sought loans from an MFI and an expensive moneylender, as well as family and neighbours, until the remittances arrived, demonstrating another critical element of the housing finance ecosystem: the sprawling system of informal credit.

Box 2.1 Microfinance for WASH and energy[6]

A house is more than mere shelter. Basic services are what makes a home suitable for the 21st century: electricity, clean water, a flush toilet, clean cookstove. Unfortunately, such services are greatly lacking and can leave people vulnerable to health crises such as the current Covid-19 pandemic. The World Bank estimated in 2012 that there were approximately 1.1 billion people worldwide without access to electricity and many more with unreliable access (World Bank, n.d.). An even greater number – 3 billion people or 41 per cent of the world's population – were still cooking with polluting fuel and stove combinations, leading to 4 million premature deaths per year (WHO, 2018).

Financial products are increasingly the path through which households are able to invest in these basic services. While WASH and energy finance lags well behind fixed asset, business, consumption, education, micro-mortgage, and agricultural loans, they do appear to be increasing in prevalence (Habitat for Humanity, 2017). Because these home improvements fit well with the incremental building model, microfinance for WASH and energy products is growing rapidly. Dozens of microfinance institutions (MFIs) in South Asia and East Africa partner with energy enterprises to offer finance for these products, typically featuring USD 100–500 loans and weekly repayments over 6–18 months, mirroring traditional microfinance lending (Microsave, 2018).

WASH loans are used for a variety of improvements including household water connections, water storage devices, water filters, wells, toilet construction, or renovation, and construction of a bathing facility. However, the flushing toilet is arguably the most important single product that can be installed at the household level. This can be a hard sell to financial institutions: a loan for a water connection/toilet may be bigger than a small business loan, but won't increase the borrower's income in the short term, and therefore such loans are perceived as more risky. In addition, it is harder to repossess a toilet or a water connection, so WASH loans offer less security for the lender.

There are several promising developments to address this long-standing challenge. WaterSHED in Cambodia is now selling the Paradise Shelter, a flat-pack toilet superstructure that can be installed quickly at a lower price than usual structures. It can also be repossessed quickly if a borrower defaults on their loan.

For the financial institution offering WASH financial products, potential benefits include deeper engagement with current clients, attracting new clients, improving client health and well-being, and healthy portfolio growth. Given their modest size, such loans are often provided to clients that are in joint-liability or self-help groups. MFIs have also conducted health education campaigns to complement the financing with community education, which increases product demand and engages community involvement (Water.org, 2015). Results from a project in Cambodia show that nearly three-fourths of water and sanitation loan recipients were new customers. Of these, about 15 per cent went on to take another loan during the programme pilot, the majority of which were for non-WASH purposes such as agriculture and small business (Water.org, 2015: 4).

Energy finance is similarly undergoing rapid change and growth, with a proliferation of new technologies, providers, and payment/finance models. Among these, solar home systems that provide lighting and charging capabilities are growing to meet energy demand in communities without reliable access to grid electricity. In this space, two models are making the greatest inroads: partnerships between energy providers and MFIs, and direct pay-as-you-go (PAYGO) financing. Across South Asia, many MFIs now offer energy loans in partnership with a manufacturer or supplier. In Africa, solar energy providers offer their products through PAYGO financing – a combination of instalment purchase and prepaid usage. The system's ability to be switched on and off remotely allows providers to link payments directly to energy use. The easy (often do-it-yourself) installation and relative portability of these systems is well-suited to finance via small microloans.

Hawala is not the only means of sending or receiving remittances. Many providers, including digital money services, compete for this enormous and rapidly growing market. In 2015, individuals sent USD 441 billion in personal remittances across borders through formal channels (World Bank, 2016: 34). This figure does not include domestic remittances, nor does it include informal channels. Housing is one of the top uses for remittances and it is likely that in many developing countries, remittances contribute more to housing than does any other financial product (Nepal Rastra Bank, 2012). But using remittances for housing is not always easy, and there is a great opportunity for remittance-based products that reduce the cost and uncertainty of using them for housing. Indeed, many microfinance loans, including housing loans, incorporate remittance income as part of the loan assessment, thus facilitating the use of irregular remittances for housing. However, more work could be done with respect to savings products or short-term bridge loans that are explicitly aimed at making remittances easier to use for housing.

Informal finance

In developing countries, all of the systems of finance mentioned above operate alongside a parallel system of informal finance. This system exists everywhere but its importance is greater in poorer countries with less financial inclusion. There are numerous examples of rotating savings clubs and associations, moneyguards, informal building societies, burial associations, and other ways poor communities have developed to manage their finances in the best way they can. The landmark study *Portfolios of the Poor* found that housing is the second-most common use of funds accumulated in this manner (Collins et al., 2009: 108).[7] The book is aimed at actors in the formal system, but recognizing the role that informal finance plays in the lives of poor households is critical to devising effective products and services. Competition is not necessarily limited to the other banks or MFIs in town, it could be a wealthy relative, local moneylender, or a savings group.

Insurance

After loans and remittances, the most common financial product for housing is insurance. In well-developed mortgage markets, insurance against fire, storm damage, and other housing risk is nearly always required as part of the mortgage contract, mitigating risk for the lender. This is not the case for either micro-mortgages or housing microfinance loans, which may require insurance on the borrower's life, but almost never on the property being financed, despite the fact that rebuilding or even repairing a seriously damaged home can pose a massive, perhaps even insurmountable, shock to the household. That alone is a significant argument for bundling home insurance with housing loans, in much the same way as credit life insurance.

There are some notable examples where this is already happening. In the Philippines, massive typhoons that regularly batter the islands can be enormously destructive. In response, the Philippine MFI Taytay Sa Kauwagan, Inc (TSKI) implemented a bundled insurance product to its clients, providing payouts in the case of death and severe home damage. The programme proved its value when TSKI, with its insurance partner MicroEnsure, paid out EUR 5.2 million to over 37,000 households whose homes were severely damaged or destroyed, following the catastrophic landing of Typhoon Haiyan in 2013 (Mendelson, 2015). However, such examples of effective housing insurance provided to poor households are unfortunately rare.

Savings

Like insurance, inclusive savings is not so much a story of what is, but rather what could be. As will be recounted in Chapter 3, saving for housing is a widespread phenomenon among poor households, mainly through the piecemeal purchase of construction materials over time until the household has gathered enough to launch the next phase of building. This process is expensive and inefficient, exposing the household to loss through material degradation and theft, while simultaneously missing the substantial discounts of bulk purchasing. Here, as in so many other instances, the poor end up paying more for less.

Despite the apparent need, experiments to offer voluntary saving products tailored for housing have not been successful. Compulsory saving, however, is a feature of many housing microfinance products. For example, before receiving a loan, a client may be required to make a set of periodic, fixed-sized savings deposits. These deposits establish the ability to make subsequent loan repayments and also enable the lender to use the savings as collateral for the loan. Nevertheless, such compulsory deposits only reinforce the credit-oriented approach to housing microfinance. Better designed and more effective voluntary savings schemes for housing remain essentially non-existent.

Funding

The three main sources of funding available for inclusive housing finance are:

- commercial (banks, investment funds, capital markets actors, and a large number of other investors seeking a commercial rate of return);
- social and development investors (the broad 'impact' investment community, bilateral and multilateral development banks, foundations, and other investors with a social or development purpose);
- government bodies (national housing funds the purpose of which is to refinance or otherwise provide financing to banks and other housing lenders).

To understand how the supply of housing finance meets demand, it is necessary to consider the types of funding available for on-lending. These will be covered in detail in Chapter 5, but in broad terms, one can consider four types of funding that a financial institution could use for housing loans: deposits, equity, debt, and asset sales (including securitization and similar transactions). Other instruments such as guarantees and loss-sharing agreements, while not funding per se, can reduce a lender's risk and help it to secure funding.

Each of these may provide funding in different ways. Indeed, the diversity of different funding structures and approaches in housing is too great to cover fully in this book. However, the key types of funding are described briefly below.

Deposits

For banks and other financial institutions with a deposit licence, deposits constitute one of the primary mechanisms for funding all loans, including housing. Deposits have many advantages as a source of funds: cost of funds is low, they come in local currency, and the market for raising deposits is typically stable. But deposits also come with significant challenges. Primary among these is a substantial risk of asset–liability mismatch given the longer tenors needed for housing loans, especially micro-mortgages. Fixed-term deposits of more than a few years are unusual, and demand deposits can be withdrawn at any time, creating not only potentially severe liquidity risk resulting from an unexpected decline in deposits, but also the complex challenge of managing operations in environments where interest rates are volatile.

Nevertheless, for those that are able to manage this risk, the opportunity is significant. Delta Brac Housing Finance Corporation Ltd (DBH) in Bangladesh, has been funded almost entirely through deposits for over 20 years. DBH has retained its AAA rating for over a decade, even as its balance sheet shows very large disparities in the maturities of its assets and liabilities. Most of its deposits are below one year, while its housing loans are mostly above five years' maturity. It is a rare, if instructive example. While many microfinance institutions rely on deposits for a part of their funding, using deposits to fund housing loans remains a largely under-utilized opportunity.[8]

Debt

The most common type of funding for inclusive housing finance is debt. All types of investors – commercial banks and investment funds, social and development investors, or even government entities, including specialized housing finance facilities – channel the bulk of their housing funds through various debt instruments.

One reason debt is advantageous is because, as a liability, it largely mirrors the loan portfolio on the asset side of the balance sheet, making asset–liability matching a straightforward process. Both feature fixed funding amounts, fixed repayment schedules, and clearly defined repayment terms and interest. Institutions can ensure that both the debt and the loans it finances feature either fixed or variable interest rates linked to the same reference index, if not they can be hedged. Matching debt with loan portfolio maturities all but eliminates the liquidity risk present with deposits.

Debt can also be a way for governments and development investors to funnel subsidies to housing finance institutions. A few percentage points shaved off the interest rate can make a significant difference in loan affordability to the borrower, and can be a means to cover the high cost of developing new housing loans. Such subsidized loans usually come with a set of targeting requirements that providers are required to fulfil in order to qualify for the subsidized funds. This type of lending reduces the open-ended liabilities, large administrations, and other costs often associated with government social programmes. For examples of such lending, see AFD's funding of Fondo MiVivienda and NHB India discussed in Chapter 5.

One major challenge with debt is the foreign exchange risk that is often created when it crosses borders. This is an especially common problem for social and development investors based in upper-income countries that fund housing finance in lower-income countries. Currencies are inherently volatile and can be especially so for some developing countries, making hedging instruments to mitigate the risk particularly expensive. Passing on those hedging costs to end-borrowers can effectively price them out of the market. To avoid assuming foreign exchange risk, lenders in some markets offer housing loans in foreign currency. While this makes the perceived interest rate quite affordable, the risks it creates for borrowers can be substantial.

Equity

While debt represents the vast majority of social and development investment in housing finance, it is equity investment that allows for the greatest degree of influence and catalytic effect. Well-capitalized financial institutions present a much lower risk to potential creditors than poorly capitalized ones. As a result, better capitalization opens debt funding opportunities from a broader range of sources, including commercial ones, and at lower rates. It is not uncommon for equity investments to be leveraged with debt funding by a factor of four or more.

Equity investment also often comes with significant influence on the investee's strategy and operations, since holders of significant equity can exert control by appointing directors to the company's board and its various committees. Such control makes seeking equity more than just a funding decision; it is also a decision about an institution's mission and values. Equity should thus be pursued with a clear focus.

Finally, an equity investment is nearly always long term. Most equity investors have a horizon of at least five years, and often closer to ten years.

At the end of the investment period, many investors choose to exit by selling their equity to other shareholders and in some cases, even to the investee itself. For some investors, such as closed-end funds with limited time spans, exits are built into the process. For others, it may be on option exercised based on changed circumstances. Still others choose not to exit at all, essentially becoming near-permanent owners. The exit is also an investor's only real opportunity to cash out and realize profits, if any. The sole exception is shareholder dividends paid over the course of the investment, though for young organizations these are rare.

Because of all these factors, equity is a particularly valuable opportunity for investors with strong social and development objectives. The cases of investors presented in Chapter 5, such as Caspian Advisors and IFC, demonstrate the various ways equity investment can play an important catalytic role in the development of both their investees and the broader housing finance sector in the country.

Asset sales

Sale of loans to other parties is another important vehicle to finance lending, usually through some form of bundling. The most well-known form for such sales is asset-backed securitization, but other structures exist including covered bonds, direct sale or assignment, and other variations.

Securitization and covered bonds account for a large share (and in some rich countries even a large majority) of funding for housing finance, especially home mortgages. This is because they are efficient mechanisms for transforming the cash flows from loans over many years to investors seeking long-term assets, such as pension funds and large insurers. A well-established system of recorded liens and an efficient foreclosure system is necessary to provide the high degree of security required by investors in securities or direct assets.

In developing countries, such mortgage systems are rarely as well developed or may not exist at all. The capital markets needed to trade securities are also insufficiently developed. For this reason, securitization remains a small part of the picture in inclusive housing finance. However, the practice of direct portfolio assignment and some securitization in both the housing finance and microfinance sectors in India provides a possible example of future developments, and this is explored in more detail in Chapter 5.

Enabling environment

Finally, the organization of the ecosystem is largely determined by its enabling environment – the specific regulations governing land, building, and finance, as well as the broader monetary policies and macro-economic management that affect housing finance.

Economic environment

The broadest of these policies are far removed from housing and influence the economy at large. At the macro-economic level, factors such as currency stability, inflation, and interest rates shape how a country's financial sector interacts with the housing market. In extreme cases like hyperinflation, it may leave the sector unable to respond at all to housing finance demand. But even more modest and relatively common situations, such as lack of currency stability or moderate inflation, may limit the appetite of financial institutions to borrow from foreign sources, or push them to lend in a stable foreign currency, thus saddling borrowers with complex currency risks.

Inflation can play a similar role even with local currency funding. Once inflation crosses into double-digits, it can dampen the willingness of investors to put up the long-term funds that are needed for housing finance, while simultaneously reducing the affordability of those loans to the end-clients. In such a scenario, housing loans are often among the least attractive products from the lender's perspective.

It certainly helps to have a growing economy where gains are spread broadly, including to poor households, which gives them the extra income needed to invest in housing. Similarly, policies that enable and perhaps even encourage citizens to seek work abroad, remitting a significant share of their earnings back home, can be a major stimulant to home improvements, as discussed above. However, this is more applicable to temporary rather than permanent migrants: people are more likely to invest in homes in which they plan to eventually live.

Financial regulation

Like the laws and regulations on land and building, those affecting the financial sector, and housing finance in particular, set the parameters within which the market can operate. Unfortunately, well-intentioned rules meant to protect the stability of the financial sector may have the unintended consequence of making housing finance inaccessible to many poor households.

For example, when risk capital levels are set higher for loans without real estate collateral, they add a real cost burden for institutions that serve poor families unable to produce the formal property titles required by such regulations. Yet these regulations are remarkably common and are in many cases responsible for keeping the supply of formal housing finance far below the levels demanded by a growing and urbanizing populace. In India, for example, central bank regulations limit non-microfinance lending (including housing loans) by registered microfinance institutions to 15 per cent of their total loan portfolios. As a result, inclusive housing finance is dominated by specialized housing finance institutions; the role of other financial providers is limited. Such a regulation creates a preference for mortgages over housing

---

Box 2.2 Bolivia

In 2013, the Bolivian government introduced a new financial system law that sought to encourage the financial sector to pursue social objectives as laid out in the government's poverty reduction plan. The law established that financial institutions must allocate 60 per cent of total lending to productive loans and housing. Further, the law required that a portion of financial intermediaries' profits be channelled into a guarantee fund to replace and/or complement the down-payment that most financial institutions require from clients applying for a housing loan.

For the most part, regulated financial institutions have met these targets, and the number of loans for housing (mortgages) has materially increased. Nevertheless, these new rules have forced financial institutions to adjust their activities in order to remain sustainable, and the results have been mixed. To comply with the required quotas, lenders are forced to take on more risk and arrears have increased in the sector as a result. If this trend accelerates, it will not be long before the banks' risk units start signalling the need to take corrective actions.

While mortgage loans have increased, progressive construction loans to very small clients have been reduced. Indeed, to meet the required targets, microfinance and similar institutions offering smaller loans have increased loan sizes to compensate for mandated lower interest rates. As a result, access to credit for very low-income families, including progressive housing loans, has been curtailed.

---

microfinance loans. This is discussed at more length in the India deep dive at the end of this chapter.

Naturally, regulations affecting inclusive housing finance can also be enabling. Preferential treatment may include lower capital requirements and tax advantages linked to loans targeting low-income populations. Governments can also set targets for housing finance, encouraging a greater flow of funds into the sector, as happened in Bolivia (see Box 2.2).[9]

Subsidy

To encourage financial institutions to provide lower-cost loans to clients, governments might allocate land on a subsidized basis or offer below-market funding. Subsidy can also be provided directly to homeowners and, when done properly, can catalyse additional funding from financial institutions. Even a small subsidy to a poor family can mean the difference between a basic home and no home at all. No less importantly, subsidies can lay the foundation for an effective housing microfinance loan or similar product. However, ensuring that subsidy is appropriately sized and properly targeted is critical. Overly generous subsidies can be misdirected through corruption to wealthy, well-connected households.

An increasingly popular tool governments deploy to expand inclusive housing finance is establishing wholesale refinancing institutions. Sometimes these are capitalized entirely by government funds while in other cases via public–private partnerships or in collaboration with international development agencies. These wholesale institutions provide local currency refinancing to banks, microfinance institutions, specialized housing finance providers, and others, often under carefully set out guidelines that govern the types of loans that can be refinanced, the target clients or geographic areas, as well as governance and operational requirements the recipient institutions are required to observe.

While they don't issue regulations per se, the large scale and below-market funding of wholesale funds is often sufficient to establish de facto standards that most housing finance providers follow. In fact, it is common to see a segmentation of the housing loan market, where 'qualifying' loans make up one segment with its own pricing levels and competition, and loans that don't qualify making up other segments with a more diverse set of characteristics.

Summary

The inclusive housing finance ecosystem is a highly complex environment, with multiple actors playing multiple roles. All can have an impact on the housing finance options available to poor households. This includes factors that are far removed from finance, such as the laws governing land or regulations that affect building.

Within the area of finance itself multiple layers are at work: products and the providers that offer them, available funding, the enabling environment, and regulations that govern housing finance, as well as the broader economy. Amidst all this complexity, the informal finance market operating in the background provides many of the financial solutions that poor households use to build their homes.

The remainder of this book will delve in detail into the households at the centre of the system, housing products and providers, and funding flows, providing many examples along the way. However, it helps to keep in mind that these are part of the broader ecosystem of housing finance that is usually invisible, but essential nevertheless. To end this chapter, we turn to India's housing finance ecosystem as a case in point.

Case study: An overview of the affordable housing ecosystem in India[10]

India accounts for 1/6th of the world's population and is undergoing the largest rural-to-urban migration in the world. In the 10-year period from 2008 to 2018, India's cities increased by nearly 100 million residents, and the urbanization rate is expected to continue in the years ahead (United Nations, 2018). In 2014, a study estimated the housing shortage in India to be 59 million units, and it is expected to grow to 90 million by 2022 (KPMG India, 2014). The problem is not limited to urbanization and growth, but also the quality of existing housing. In 2017, 40 per cent of India's population lacked basic sanitation facilities, much of it in rural areas (WHO/UNICEF, 2019).

These worrying trends inspired a series of government efforts to address the problem, most recently 'Housing for All by 2022' launched in 2015.

But public policies to encourage affordable housing in India go back to well before then. They have shaped a market that features a range of both socially and commercially motivated actors working to provide housing finance, and ultimately housing itself, to millions of underserved Indian families.

The policies that shape the enabling environment in India can be grouped in four categories: economic environment, land policies, financial regulation, and subsidy.

Economic environment

India has enjoyed cumulative annual growth of 7.3 per cent between 2000 and 2018, among the highest in the world.[11] Inflation has been moderate and there were no sudden devaluations or currency shocks during this period. The monetary and economic environment has been quite favourable to an expansion of credit, resulting in private sector credit nearly doubling as a share of the economy over this period.[12] For affordable housing finance, this has been a propitious environment for growth.

Land policies

Generally, India scores rather low on metrics like ease of registering property.[13] However, this has been changing. Digital land and property records have been introduced by several state governments as part of a move towards 'ease of doing business'. Even more important for housing finance, policies have made it possible for land to be used as collateral, even for relatively small loans. The 2002 Securitisation and Reconstruction of Financial Assets and Enforcement of Security Interest (SARFAESI) Act created a mechanism for effective and reliable foreclosure of properties on defaulted loans issued by banks and housing finance companies (HFCs). The subsequent establishment of the Central Registry of Securitisation, Asset Reconstruction and Security Interest of India (CERSAI) in 2011 provided the institutional and process backbone for registering and tracking property collateral. The CERSAI data portal facilitates appraisals and valuation by lenders, while also preventing them from unknowingly issuing multiple loans against the same collateral.

More recently, the Real Estate Regulation & Development Act (RERA) adopted in 2016 provides for registration of projects undertaken by builders and sets a number of standards and requirements. RERA has also created a mandatory requirement for title insurance, which is currently being implemented.

Financial regulation

A wide range of regulations and financial sector infrastructure have further enabled affordable housing finance in India. Chapter 5 discusses the key role of the National Housing Bank (NHB) and its incubation of affordable housing finance companies. The role of NHB is complemented by two important initiatives: the Credit Risk Guarantee Fund Trust for Low Income Housing and the India Mortgage Guarantee Corporation (IMGC). The former enables lenders to purchase a credit guarantee that covers up to 90 per cent of loan loss for qualified housing loans to low income households. It was established in 2012, funded by the government of India and participating state governments, and operated by NHB (see Chapter 5 for details). The IMGC, created in 2013, has a broad mandate to provide mortgage insurance, including for affordable housing loans. It is the first mortgage guaranty company in the country and is a joint venture of the IFC, NHB, Asian Development Bank (ADB), and Genworth US.

Several regulations explicitly promote lending to poor and excluded households in India, including for affordable housing. One of these, the priority sector mandate, requires regulated banks to devote 40 per cent of their credit portfolios to specified segments, including affordable housing finance. This is a key aspect of India's financial inclusion policy. Designation of affordable housing as an 'infrastructure' investment is another important policy encouragement that brings a number of accompanying tax benefits. The result of these designations is to encourage local, commercial funding for qualifying affordable housing lending, which is insulated against the kind of foreign currency risks that plague similar loans in many other countries.

At the same time, some regulations specific to microfinance institutions (MFIs) have had a limiting effect on housing finance. Following the Andhra Pradesh microfinance crisis in 2010, a new category of financial institution was created: the non-bank finance company MFI (NBFC-MFI). Under this licence, at least 85 per cent of an NBFC-MFI's portfolio must be composed of microloans with terms appropriate for short-term working capital but inconsistent with housing microfinance. This requirement effectively forced MFIs to focus on microcredit, stifling any efforts on their part to diversify into housing microfinance.

More recently, the central bank issued a new type of licence, the small finance bank (SFB), which allows licensees to expand into new activities, including taking deposits. Crucially for housing, the regulatory conditions of an SFB are encouraging to the affordable housing finance sector, both housing microfinance and micro-mortgage. During 2016–2017, most of the country's leading MFIs were granted the new SFB licence and several of them have expanded their housing loan programmes.[14] The Reserve Bank of India (RBI)'s requirement that SFBs lend at least 75 per cent of their loan book to priority sectors provides a built-in encouragement for individual housing loans up to Rs. 3 million (USD 42,000), which are treated as priority-sector lending.

Subsidy

There is a suite of government initiatives and policies that provide an important element of direct support to builders, lenders, and low-income households. These range from tax incentives to interest rate subsidies to direct financial grants. The number of programmes is large and in addition to national government individual state governments have programmes as well.

On the tax side, there are several advantages given to housing credit. To begin with, builders enjoy a tax exemption on all profits from affordable housing units built under schemes approved by the central and state governments. There are additional tax benefits that allow households to sell property and use the proceeds to purchase up to two properties, without attracting capital gains tax.

Under the rubric of 'Housing for All by 2022', a number of schemes are linked directly to housing loans. Most prominent among these is the Prime Minister's Housing Programme (PMAY) that itself features multiple streams. Among these, the Credit Linked Subsidy Scheme (CLSS) is the most directly linked to housing finance. Under CLSS, the government of India provides an interest subsidy of up to 6.5 per cent of the loan amount to qualified households, with the largest subsidy reserved for households in poverty. Smaller subsidies of 3–4 per cent are available for households near poverty (middle-income groups). The CLSS also specifies maximum loan amounts and property sizes for each subsidy tier, up to a maximum of INR 1.2 million (USD 15,000) and 200 m². The CLSS subsidies are implemented by the National Housing Bank and its participating housing lenders, including HFCs, banks, and microfinance institutions, who document the eligibility of recipient borrowers.

The PMAY initiative also features schemes where the government of India provides direct grants in partnership with state governments and private developers to redevelop slums and build affordable housing in both urban and rural areas. The largest of these, the Indira Awas Yojna (IAY) grant, was launched in 1985 and from inception through June 2017 has facilitated the construction of 35.1 million houses. In 2015–2016, IAY was rolled into the new PMAY-G scheme, which now provides up to Rs 130,000 (USD 1,500) for qualifying home construction. In addition, recognizing the eligibility limitations of the PMAY scheme, in 2018 the government of India also launched the Rural Housing Interest Subsidy Scheme (RHISS) that provides an interest subsidy to all rural households not eligible under PMAY-G. Any household borrowing under RHISS is eligible for an interest subsidy of 3 per cent on the first Rs. 200,000 (USD 2,500) of the loan amount. Like the other credit subsidy schemes, this too is administered by the NHB, working with a broad group of housing lenders.

Finally, the NHB provides sub-market wholesale funding and refinancing to housing lenders, as described in more detail in Chapter 5.

Housing microfinance or micro-mortgages?

One of the most notable outcomes of this broad mix of policies and financial sector infrastructure has been the minor role that housing microfinance has played in India, while micro-mortgages have taken the primary role in the sector. As will be described extensively in Chapter 4, housing microfinance is a product that typically finances incremental home building, funding components of the house at each phase of construction; a process that takes several years or more. In this way, it largely reflects the typical building practices of poor families around the world. In India, housing microfinance loans are not legally secured by land collateral.

Micro-mortgages on the other hand are fully collateralized by the property, fully and effectively enforceable in court (see the description of SARFAESI above). However, unlike traditional mortgages, micro-mortgages are regularly issued to borrowers with informal incomes that would otherwise make them ineligible for a bank-issued mortgage. Having the security of legally enforceable collateral allows lenders to make longer-term loans, and thus provide loan amounts large enough to cover the purchase or construction of an entire home, rather than settling for incremental building. Even if the cost of loan assessment for an informal income household is greater, the larger loan size spread over a longer period still allows the lender to charge an interest rate that is significantly lower than that associated with housing microfinance. This innovation has unlocked the mortgage market to the millions of poor and near-poor Indian households that had previously been excluded.

A comparison between housing microfinance and micro-mortgage loan features is provided in Table 2.1. Though there will be product variations by lender, this is fairly representative of the key differences between the two types of financing:

With demand for affordable housing continuing to grow for the foreseeable future, the housing finance ecosystem will continue to evolve. The policy foundations and enabling environment established over the past decade has served the sector well. With a mix of local commercial funds and a broad range of providers on the demand side (banks, HFCs, MFIs, and NGOs), and builders in public and private sectors on the supply side, India is well positioned to expand the contours of affordable housing in the country.

Table 2.1 Housing microfinance and micro-mortgages in India

Loan features	Housing microfinance (unsecured)	Micro-mortgage (secured)
Purpose of the loan	Home improvement, minor repairs and addition	Purchase or construction
Security	Guarantor; no hard security	Property mortgage
Average loan amount	USD 1,000–2,000	USD 7,000–12,000
Average loan tenor	24–36 months	120–180 months
Average interest rate	20–22% p.a.	13–15% p.a.
Annual income (range)	USD 1,500–2,500	USD 4,000–7,000
Loan to value ratio (range)	70–80% of project cost	40–85% of property value
Market size (Dec 2017)	<Rs 50 billion (USD 650 million)[15]	Rs 220 billion (USD 2.5 trillion)*[16]

Notes

1. Custom data acquired via website. See also World Bank (2016) <www.worldbank.org/en/news/infographic/2016/05/13/housing-for-all-by-2030>.
2. We use demand and cost interchangeably here, although from an economic perspective much of this would be considered latent demand: estimates of the cost of improving the homes of those who would like to make such improvements without consideration for their ability to do so financially. For example, if renovation to Protima's home to bring it up to standard would cost USD 2,000 but she can only afford USD 500, the demand would be USD 2000 (USD 500 actual demand + USD 1500 latent demand). In this way cost = demand.
3. The specific type of title acceptable for mortgage finance varies by jurisdiction and institution. For example, a financial institution may accept a lower level of title documentation for loans it holds on its own books, while to be sold or refinanced loans may require the highest level documentation.
4. Generally land rights are tied to ownership but in some jurisdictions long-term leasehold is the norm and acceptable.
5. See, for example, Chiquier, Loic and Michael Lea (2009) *Housing Finance Policy in Emerging Markets*. World Bank.
6. Contributed by Sam Mendelson.
7. Land and building accounted for 21 per cent of the primary uses of large sums accumulated by study participants (Collins et al., Table 4.5, p. 108).
8. In some countries, such as the member countries of the West African Economic and Monetary Union, the ability to use short-term assets to fund long-term liabilities is limited by regulation.
9. Contributed by Maria Teresa Morales, Habitat for Humanity Latin America.
10. Based on material provided by R.V. Verma and Mona Kachhwaha.
11. IMF World Economic Outlook, April 2019, gross domestic product (constant prices, national currency).
12. World Bank, domestic credit to private sector (percentage of GDP) grew from 28 per cent in 2000 to 50 per cent in 2018.
13. The World Bank Doing Business Report 2020 ranked India 154th out of 190 countries on the metric of 'Registering Property', which measures the time and cost required to register a commercial warehouse. However, because of differences with residential property, these results may not be indicative for residential construction.
14. Seven of the ten institutions that were licensed as SFBs were MFIs. The other three included two NBFCs and one local area bank.
15. Estimate provided by Caspian Impact Investment Advisers, including loans issued by MFIs and HFCs.
16. Estimate from *State of the Low-Income Housing Finance Market Report* Market size refers to HFCs only.

References

Collins, D., Morduch, J., Rutherford, S. and Ruthven, O. (2009) *Portfolios of the Poor: How the World's Poor Live on $2 a Day*, Princeton University Press, Princeton, NJ.

Daphnis, F. and Ferguson, B. (2004) *Housing Microfinance: A Guide to Practice*, Kumarian Press Inc., Bloomfield, CT.

Das, C., Karamchandani, A. and Thuard, J. (2018) *Report: State of the Low-Income Housing Finance Market*, FSG <https://www.fsg.org/publications/state-low-income-housing-finance-market-2018#downloadarea>. Market size refers to HFCs only.

Habitat for Humanity (2017) *The 2016–2017 State of Housing Microfinance: Understanding the Business Case for Housing Microfinance*, Terwilliger Center for Innovation in Shelter, Habitat for Humanity, Atlanta, GA.

KPMG India (2014) *Funding the Vision: 'Housing for All by 2022'* <https://assets.kpmg/content/dam/kpmg/pdf/2014/08/KPMG-NAREDCO-Funding-the-vision.pdf>.

McKinsey & Company (2014) *A Blueprint for Addressing the Global Affordable Housing Challenge*, McKinsey Global Institute.

Mendelson, S. (2015) *Microfinance in Post-Disaster, Post-Conflict Areas and Fragile States: Resilience and Responsibility*, European Dialogue #9, European Microfinance Platform, Luxembourg.

Microsave (2018) *Financing WASH: Key Considerations for MFIs*, Briefing Note #152 <www.microsave.net/wp-content/uploads/2018/10/BN_152_Financing_WASH_Key_Considerations_for_MFIs.pdf>.

United Nations (2018) *World Urbanization Prospects: The 2018 Revision*, custom data acquired via website. Department of Economic and Social Affairs, Population Division, New York.

Water.org (2015) *Financing Water and Sanitation for the Poor: The Role of Microfinance Institutions in Addressing the Water and Sanitation Gap*, Learning Note <www.wsp.org/sites/wsp/files/publications/WSP-Waterdotorg-Financing-WASH-for-the-Poor-Microfinance.pdf>.

WHO (2018) *Fact Sheet*, World Health Organization, Geneva <www.who.int/news-room/fact-sheets/detail/household-air-pollutionand-health>.

WHO/UNICEF Joint Monitoring Programme (2019) 'India: Proportion of population using at least basic sanitation services, 2017' <https://data.unicef.org/country/ind/#/>.

World Bank (2016) *Migration and Remittances Factbook 2016*, World Bank Group, Washington DC.

World Bank (2016) Housing For All by 2030 infographic, World Bank Group, Washington DC <www.worldbank.org/en/news/infographic/2016/05/13/housing-for-all-by-2030>.

World Bank (no date) *SE4ALL Global Tracking Framework* <www.worldbank.org/en/topic/energy/publication/Global-Tracking-Framework-Report>.

Author biographies

Daniel Rozas is a senior microfinance expert at e-MFP and a consultant and researcher on a broad range of financial inclusion topics. Prior to his microfinance career, Daniel worked for the US mortgage investment company Fannie Mae during 2001–2008, where he had first-hand experience with the extraordinary boom-and-bust cycle that took place in the US mortgage market during this period.

Patrick McAllister finds innovative finance solutions for some of the world's most challenging problems related to poverty and inequality. His experience in housing began at the US Department of Housing and Urban Development and he was Habitat for Humanity's Asia Director of Housing Finance from 2010 to 2015. Currently, in addition to housing finance, he is focusing on the problem of plastic in the ocean.

CHAPTER 3
Do-it-yourself housing

Stuart Rutherford

Low-income households often have to do many things for themselves that richer people can easily have done for them, including managing their money and building their homes. Poorly served by formal financial services, they have to seek out and interact with informal partners to borrow or save their way to house-building. Living in this do-it-yourself economy means they often have to build incrementally, patching together finance, land, and building materials as they proceed. It often takes them many years. This chapter describes and illustrates how they go about it.

Keywords: do-it-yourself housing; low-income households; build incrementally; building materials; Bangladesh; financial inclusion; housing is a verb; remittances; non-financial services; Grameen Bank

One of the big differences in the ways that rich and poor people experience life is that poor people *do things for themselves* far more often than the rich.

Take finance: the better-off, whose income usually flows into bank accounts on a regular schedule, can have a mountain of financial tasks automated. Some of the income can be automatically diverted to savings, insurance, and pension accounts, or transferred into shares or mutual funds. Payments on the car loan, school fees, and the home mortgage will be made on time with little effort. Debts incurred through credit cards and other payment systems will be repaid on schedule, without human intervention. For each of these services, the bank maintains the detailed records that help to make future financial services easier to get. This allows the better-off to focus on the efficiency, yield, cost, and security of their financial arrangements, without needing to manage them on a day-to-day basis.

The poor enjoy none of this automation. They must focus on managing, not just monitoring, their finances. They must seek out financial partners in their family and community, assessing for themselves how safe this money-guard or that savings club is likely to be, or how difficult a creditor will prove. And they have to remember to make the payments. Those payments often come not from a regular flow of income but from irregular and uncertain returns from informal labour and self-employment. When we say that poor people are 'financially excluded' we do not mean that they engage in no financial activity; there's plenty of evidence that poor people are active users of savings and borrowing services and devices (Rutherford and

http://dx.doi.org/10.3362/9781730447681.004

Sukhwinder, 2009). To be financially excluded simply means to be excluded from the luxury of formal finance's efficiency, transparency, regularity, and automation. Poor people's finance is above all else *do-it-yourself* finance.

Housing is another field where the better-off are served while the poor are left to serve themselves. Among those who own their home, or aspire to do so, the rich are more likely to buy a complete home, at a stroke. The poor are more likely to camp for years in a part-completed dwelling that they are building for themselves, often with their own labour, buying materials as and when they can. John F.C. Turner summed it up best with the title of his classic essay based on his experience observing squatters in Peru: for the poor, 'Housing is a Verb' (Turner, 1972).[1]

The reader can see where this is heading. Finance and housing are two areas where the poor are forced to rely heavily on their own resources, making their experience very different from that of better-off people. *Housing finance needs to be understood from the perspective of the poor if it is to be improved.* Hence this chapter, in which the words of poor householders themselves, and data gleaned from close observation of their lives, are used to describe their experiences.

The do-it-yourself construction process

Many low-income people dream of building brand new homes, but few realize that dream. Most must settle for repairing and expanding their existing home. Very often these existing structures are a patchwork of construction efforts rather than the finished products of professional house builders. Though the style, materials, technology, and cost of the homes vary with location, we see this same phenomenon of incremental building around the world. Box 3.1' illustrates the process many low-income households go through, consciously or unconsciously, to house themselves and their families.[2] It also helps explain why so many of these houses look similar and use similar materials and technology despite the availability of alternatives that may seem more suited to the local environment.

This theme of adapting the building process to the family's circumstances is replicated in their financing strategies. Though shelter, like food, is fundamental to human survival, it is an intermittent, rather than an everyday, expense. Each bout of expenditure requires the accumulation of the necessary funds – a process that takes time and financial planning. In some farming communities it is not uncommon to see 'building seasons' that come in the months immediately following the harvest, when families have money to spend from the sale of their crops. For other households, it is the irregular, but relatively large, remittances from family members working abroad that can be spent on housing. But not all families can rely on such large, intermittent inflows. Instead, the accumulation of the lump sums needed for housing can be met by saving and borrowing. Such is the experience of Nikhil, described in Nikhil's story.[3]

Box 3.1 How people build

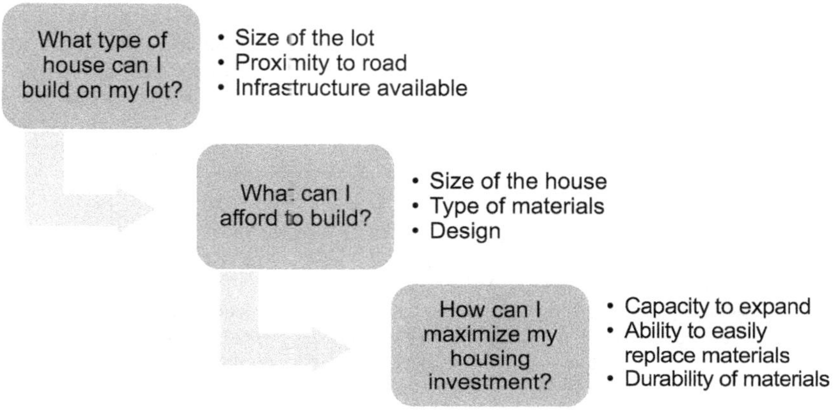

What type of house can I build on my lot?
- Size of the lot
- Proximity to road
- Infrastructure available

What can I afford to build?
- Size of the house
- Type of materials
- Design

How can I maximize my housing investment?
- Capacity to expand
- Ability to easily replace materials
- Durability of materials

Figure 3.1 How people build

What type of house can I build on my lot? Before a family even begins to build a home, there is the question of land. In urban areas of many developing countries, land is not only scarce but often poorly documented. Many of these countries are undergoing rapid urbanization, and as poor rural households migrate to cities they settle in squatter communities – dense informal settlements, often in hard-to-access locations such as hills and ravines, on government or privately owned land. Through an informal process, households 'claim' small plots on which they can begin to build. As these 'slum' communities grow, some are able to gain recognition from local government, even if not actual ownership. The risk of eviction declines and longer-term investment in housing becomes feasible. In rural areas, there are usually fewer uncertainties regarding the land, which is often either owned by the family or recognized as legitimately occupied by local communal rights.

What can I afford? Money and locally available supplies drive construction choices. In areas where infrastructure is under-developed, the absence of roads means construction materials are more costly and must often be transported by hand, over multiple trips. In slums, the ever-present risk of eviction limits the amount of investment households are willing to make in their new homes with the result that these initial dwellings are made of found materials (tarp, plastic sheeting, pallet wood) and are largely temporary in nature. The poorest rural families typically start with local materials using traditional construction techniques such as adobe/mud walls, bamboo, palm fronds, and locally harvested timber. Once sufficient funding becomes available, families seek to upgrade to the cement block and corrugated sheet roofing style that is ubiquitous in both rural and urban poor communities around the world. The result is that these homes are remarkably similar across regions and even continents, despite being built without any kind of architectural planning or design. Indeed, the building is almost always done by labourers without formal qualifications, such as a local mason or carpenter, often with additional labour provided by friends or the family itself.

How can I maximize my housing investment over time? For a poor family, a house is not a product, it is a continuous process. Usually, it is built incrementally, starting with walls (masonry, concrete blocks, mud bricks, or timber framing), then roofing (corrugated metal sheeting is especially common), and eventually windows and doors. Throughout the

(Continued)

Box 3.1 Continued

process, the home is ever-evolving and intentionally expandable, so that a second storey or a toilet may be added as the family grows and has the resources available to invest. In communities dominated by incremental building, it is common to see seemingly half-built homes, with steel bars protruding from columns or wall blocks aligned in a protruding pattern – all to facilitate the addition of another room or a second floor, like a set of Lego blocks. The building is also modular, so that, for example, a lower-quality roof can be easily replaced by a better one. The design is intrinsic to an ever-evolving home.

Nikhil's story: Patching up an old home

In Autumn 2015, Nikhil (Photo 3.1) volunteered to be a respondent in the daily financial diary project. He was working in a small biscuit factory on low pay, pounding dough in a dark and dingy room for long hours seven days a week. He was in his mid-50s, stooped and with a nervous manner. He lived with his wife and a school-aged son in a makeshift home on ancestral land that had been endlessly divided up as the generations passed. They had no farmland nor other assets besides the house and the land it stood on. The couple were repaying a microfinance loan that they had taken to help pay for his daughter's marriage. His wife, who had a few years of primary education, did her best to bring in some extra money by tutoring school children, but she rarely made more than the equivalent of USD 5 a month.[4]

Photo 3.1 Nikhil at work
Credit: Stuart Rutherford

Their priorities were straightforward: to eat enough to survive, to continue their boy's education, to pay off the debts for their daughter's marriage – and to improve their ramshackle home.

(Continued)

Nikhil's story: Continued

Photo 3.2 The old room at the rear (with new roofing), the new one in the centre, and work on the kitchen and toilet in the foreground
Credit: Shamol

Since then, building work on the home has taken place in occasional brief bursts of activity (Photo 3.2). At the start of 2016, Nikhil bought timber and bamboo and began work on a new room adjoining the old house. He didn't get very far, but in June that year he resumed, buying cement to make concrete pillars and metal sheeting for the roof and walls. The new room was almost complete. Another pause, then as 2017 began he turned to his kitchen, which had been just a lean-to shed, buying timber for a door and windows, and drilling a drinking-water pump. In August 2017 he patched up the older rooms. Finally, in early 2018, he built an outside pit latrine.

By buying the cheapest materials and doing much of the work himself, his total cost for building materials and labour amounted to only USD 1,066. Where did the money come from? A chart will help disentangle the reasons for his on-off building progress.

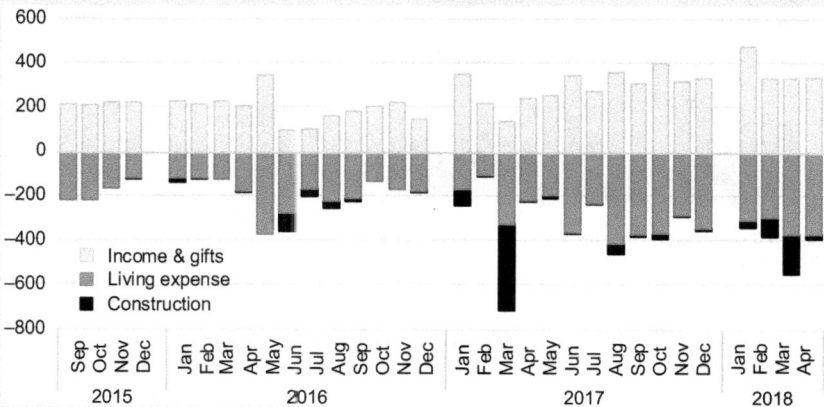

Figure 3.2 Nikhil monthly money flows

(Continued)

Nikhil's story: Continued

Figure 3.2 shows the household's income each month (above the line, unshaded). Earned income averages USD 230 a month, which for a three-person household puts it a little above the internationally recognized USD 1.90 per person per day line for extreme poverty, but they also get some gifts. Below the line (shaded) is shown their spending on everything other than construction. The construction work costs are shown in black, and the main bursts of building mentioned in the previous paragraph have been circled.

The amounts spent on construction aren't large relative to income: only the water pump drilled in March 2017 cost more than a month's income. But it is important to take account of what else was happening to Nikhil and his wife. At first they were still repaying the loan taken for their daughter's marriage. That loan was paid off in April 2016 and a few weeks later they took another large loan from the MFI, Grameen Bank. This allowed them to pay off some private debts and to spend some money that month on the building work. But just then Nikhil lost his job. Income shrank dramatically in the middle of the year, then recovered in August when he began a series of other jobs. As a result, the new MFI loan was used in part for living expenses or stored at home for security during the bumpy employment patch. By the beginning of 2017 he had settled into a very low-prestige job (serving in a tiny tea-stall) but which paid him a daily wage that accumulated to more than he had been getting at the biscuit factory. They took the plunge and dug the water pump, bathroom, and latrine (Photo 3.3).

Photo 3.3 The new toilet/bathroom
Credit: Shamol

Then came another change. Nikhil's son-in-law's parents got into trouble, and the son-in-law – now working in Dubai – asked if his wife, Nikhil's daughter, could live with Nikhil. This meant another mouth to feed, but the son-in-law sent some extra money every couple of months. It also put pressure on Nikhil to make sure that his son-in-law wouldn't be too ashamed of the home his wife was living in, and it was this that pushed him into building the new bathroom and latrine.

Nikhil's family comes from central Bangladesh, and there will be other stories from the same place because of the especially rich data, based on a set of 'financial diaries' that have been running there since mid-2015. In these 'diaries', volunteer households tell researchers about every penny that comes into or leaves their hands each day, seven days a week, over several years. Their responses to questions about why they made the transactions they did, and what the outcomes were, are recorded. As the stories show, this gives a narrative account, based on the householder's own words, and a transactional record giving the value and the date of all housing-related transactions.

Nikhil's case shows the sometimes contradictory effects of financial flows on the speed of building projects. Repaying a large MFI loan to help finance his daughter's marriage held him back from construction work for a long time. When that loan was finally paid off he took another, hoping to get going on a new room. But because he unexpectedly lost his job just at that moment, the loan had to perform as a cash reserve to ensure that the family could make it through until he got ongoing employment once again.

Such unforeseen turns are so common as to almost be a norm for households like Nikhil's. His experience illustrates one of the most common approaches to do-it-yourself housing: investing in housing when the financial situation is good, and delaying planned building when things suddenly turn for the worse. This incremental strategy for building and improving homes is ideally suited to the financial uncertainty facing poor families around the world. Nikhil's ability to repurpose a loan originally meant for home improvement to cover his living expenses when he lost his job is an excellent demonstration of the value of flexible finance.

Pieces of the financial puzzle

The child of uncertainty and flexibility is delay: for poor families, the vicissitudes of life – which more often than not mean unexpected expenses – get in the way, and building nearly always takes longer than originally planned. Sometimes what families need is a way to accelerate the process, by in effect prioritizing building over other expenses (see Bumak's story for how this prioritization works in practice). A housing microfinance loan can be a good mechanism to achieve this. By explicitly targeting housing, the loan is a way for a family to commit to a home investment they might otherwise have to wait years to accomplish. Such is the case with Bumak and Saerng from Cambodia.

Bumak and Saerng's access to formal home improvement loans has given them an advantage over Nikhil. But both started in do-it-yourself mode, with help from a formal lender arriving, if at all, later on. Bumak and Saerng saved hard and began their building work without any outside finance. This is a common pattern around the world. Owning land, or the ability to buy it from savings, is a pre-requisite to building. And most homeowners take loans only

Bumak's story: How finance speeds incremental building

Bumak and his wife, a couple from a neighbourhood outside Phnom Penh, Cambodia, lived apart from their two very young children for four years while they worked on their house (Habitat For Humanity, 2018).[5] Bumak sells ice-cream from a side-cart attached to his motorbike and his wife Saerng has a job in a garment factory. They are determined and disciplined savers and in 2013 were able to buy a plot of land and start building a new home on it. Meanwhile, they lived in rented accommodation – a single 12 square metre room. They explained that 'the room was small and in a noisy, unsafe area where there were many burglaries, so we thought it best to have the children stay with their grand-parents', something that the couple found very stressful.

They looked for ways of changing the situation and were lucky to get two short-term housing improvement loans of USD 2,000 each from HKL, a microfinance company. With these they first covered the shell of their house with metal roofing and then laid floor tiles and plastered the walls. The family was reunited and, according to son Thanat, now 10, 'There's room for us to play and I feel happy here' (Photo 3.4). Monthly repayments on the loans started at USD 120 and declined to USD 80 before repayment was completed around the end of 2017. The experience of taking formal loans has emboldened the couple: the upper floor is unplastered and used for storage, but they are now thinking of taking another loan to convert it into a bedroom.

Photo 3.4 Bumak and son
Credit: Habitat for Humanity

after having already started building from their own resources (Habitat for Humanity, 2019).

Loans are just one piece of the complex financial puzzle put together by self-builders. The fact that so many households use savings as a core part of their building strategy is something that deserves more attention from MFIs and other financial providers. Cash savings are often accumulated via informal financial devices like rotating savings clubs, and in rare cases through formal savings accounts.[6] An especially common way for families to save for housing is by purchasing building supplies such as bricks, cement, and roofing material over a period of time, whenever money is available. Once these supplies reach the required level, the household will invest in the next step of their construction, whether building themselves (like Nikhil above), or by hiring a local mason.

In behavioural economics parlance, buying building supplies in advance acts as a savings commitment device because, once purchased, that money has effectively been spent on housing and is no longer available for other uses. But this form of saving comes with downsides: storing materials over lengthy periods exposes them to weathering and degradation, as well as theft. An obvious way to avoid these downsides is to save with financial vehicles, such as savings accounts.

One promising tool for increasing formal savings of poor families has been commitment savings accounts, where clients agree to save a fixed amount each week or month. But commitment savings have yet to prove effective for housing, as shown in Box 3.2.

It should thus be no surprise that the vast majority of formal financial products used for housing are loans.[7] However, while loans are fundamental in enabling families to accelerate their building, as in the cases of Nikhil and Bumak, they come with important risks. This was the situation with the Benjamin family story (See page 52) from Cambodia.

Remittances

Loans and savings are not the only means to finance home building. As described in Chapter 2, many households rely on national and international remittances from family members. Remittances comprise an enormous source of income for many households, especially rural ones.

Box 3.2 The challenge of formal savings for housing

An experiment in Southeast Asia that offered self-builders commitment savings accounts showed that the large amounts and long terms they require were too high an obstacle for families planning home improvements (Habitat for Humanity, 2017).

During one focus group discussion, these clients – all women – readily recognized that saving was cheaper and safer because there was no need to make large interest payments on loans or store building materials. Despite that, nearly all felt that they were unlikely to save the large amounts needed through the scheme. Many chose instead to purchase building materials over time, while others took out loans, both formal and informal.

One woman put it this way: 'With a loan, I know I will pay!' leading to nods of agreement from others. What the women were essentially saying is that no amount of reminders, commitments, or incentives can approach the degree of compulsion that comes with loan repayments, where delinquency brings social pressure from group members, a damaged credit history, or even the threat of legal proceedings.

The Benjamin family story: The risks of over-indebtedness

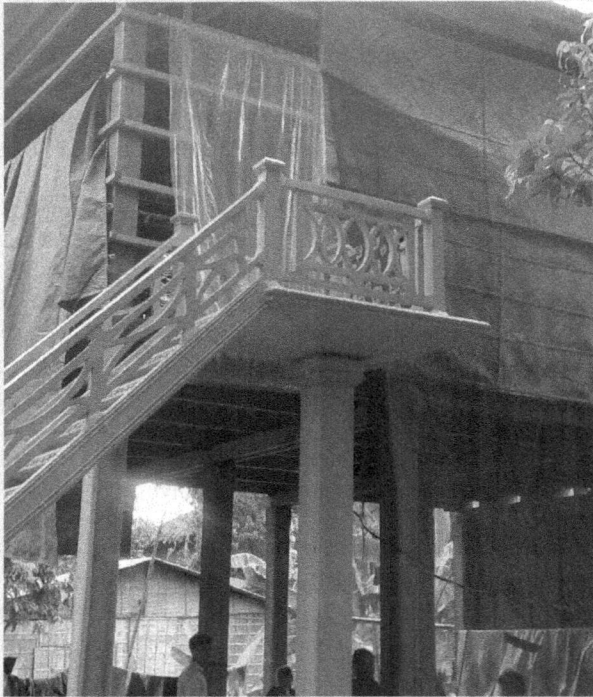

Photo 3.5 The Benjamin house
Credit: Daniel Rozas

Like many in the village, the Benjamin family worked with bamboo for their livelihood. A few years ago they began borrowing from MFIs to buy bamboo, first a USD 1,000 loan, which they repaid, and then a USD 2,000 loan from the same MFI. The monthly payments for this were a little over USD 200. Their borrowing continued to increase when they borrowed USD 3,000 from another lender, with the loan to the first still outstanding. In total, they had accumulated close to USD 5,000 in debt, with monthly payments of over USD 500. Then their business began to run into difficulties. The deliveries of bamboo became delayed, and the resulting cashflow shortage made it impossible for the Benjamins to repay their loans. At first they borrowed USD 500 from a village lender to prevent them from missing their loan payments. Soon, however, they fell behind on their MFI loans and seeing no way out, two months later they sold their house.

The sale yielded USD 15,000, with which the family could clear its debts. But now they had no home. For nearly two years, the Benjamin family lived with one of their parents outside the village, yet they did not give up.

Six months ago they bought a smaller plot of land in the village and built a new home. In all, the new home cost them USD 8,000, which they could afford using the remaining money from the sale of their old home. Both the land and the house are smaller than what they had, but they're happy to be debt-free. The house is not yet finished, with one of the walls still waiting to be completed. But the Benjamins refuse to take a loan to do it. They'll wait until they can save up the money (Rozas, 2016).

Panna's story: Remittances as housing finance

Panna is a cheerful woman in her early 30s with two children in school. In early 2016 she took on a new responsibility: supervising the construction of a family home. Her husband, Oni, is working in Singapore, and the house is being built with the money he remits to his wife.

Their home-building, however, is just the latest episode in a scheme that Oni's family has been working on for many years. His father was a dirt-poor farmer and when he died, in 1997, his four sons continued to live together as a joint family, sharing all income and expenses. But with three of the brothers already married, the old family home was too small to accommodate four growing families. So they decided to sell some of the farm land, buy a homestead plot and build a new structure divisible into four separate homes. By that time one of Oni's brothers had a job in Singapore as a carpenter and was sending home remittances, so they were full of confidence.

Things looked even better when Oni, helped by his brother, also got a Singapore job. Just before leaving he married Panna; he was 35 and she was 15. Both brothers in Singapore sent money home to their eldest brother, a rickshaw driver who continued to run things as the head of a joint family. But no accounts were kept and development of the plot was continually delayed. Money went instead into patching up the old house and adding two extra rooms to it. Then two of the wives needed expensive medical treatment. Many children were born, and additional money was lost in loans to family members.

In early 2014 Oni's brother, with whom he was working in Singapore, was injured in a fall during home leave and never went back to Singapore. By that time all they had achieved was the reinforced concrete foundation for the proposed new structure. There was no money left for more construction, said the family head. The brothers agreed to 'separate' the joint family and go their own ways. From then on Oni began to send his remittances directly to Panna, usually through the informal 'hundi' (or 'hawala') system.[8]

In late 2015 Panna became one of the 'diarists' in the Hrishipara Daily Diaries Project, so from that date on she kept complete records of all her daily transactions. For example, from November 2015 to the end of March 2018, she received 448,000 taka in 29 separate remittances. At the market exchange rate that is the equivalent of USD 5,460, or just over USD 14,000 (expressed in purchasing power parity, PPP). This made her, in the eyes of her neighbours, 'rich'.

The brothers agreed how to carve up the 'new' plot of land. Oni got almost a third of it and registered it in his name. He came home on leave to arrange for plans to be drawn up, and in March 2016 Panna made her first building-related purchases, for sand and bricks. Table 3.1 shows the construction-related expenses, which totalled 388,710 taka (86 per cent of all the remittances she received in the period). Table 3.1 also hints at the management burden that Panna took on, which, she says 'made her nervous', though she had the support and advice of the 'Singapore' brother-in-law, a carpenter.

Table 3.1 Construction expenses, March 2016 – April 2018, taka

23/03/2016	1,500	Sand
30/03/2016	14,500	Brick purchase
30/03/2016	100	Mason
07/04/2016	1,800	Sand carrying charge
07/04/2016	3,000	Brick breaking
09/04/2016	6,000	Mason
16/04/2016	4,000	Mason
19/04/2016	5,000	Mason

(Continued)

Panna's story: Continued

07/05/2016	10,500	Cement
07/05/2016	17,300	Rod
07/05/2016	45,000	Brick
07/05/2016	3,000	Mason
08/05/2016	2,000	Screw
14/05/2016	5,000	Mason
26/05/2016	16,000	Brick purchase
30/05/2016	1,500	Polyethylene
30/05/2016	90,000	Mason
10/06/2016	820	Screws
01/09/2016	10,000	Cement
10/11/2016	50	Lock and key
31/01/2017	50	Paint
21/02/2017	18,000	Cement
20/06/2017	100	Tub
05/10/2017	40	Nails
05/10/2017	150	Timber
06/10/2017	800	Timber
24/01/2018	17,000	Bricks
27/01/2018	51,000	Bricks
13/03/2018	11,000	Cement
15/03/2018	3,000	Mason
18/03/2018	34,000	Bricks
18/03/2018	6,500	Mason
20/03/2018	10,000	Mason

There is another story told in Table 3.1: that the building process was not a smooth continuum. Work slowed down in the second half of the year, not just because of the seasonal rains, but because Panna had to manage other family crises. On 20 June 2017 her son fell and drove a bamboo stick into his eye and needed repeated treatments.

Moreover, the flow of remittances didn't always match the rhythm of the building work. In May 2016 her brother-in-law urged her to complete the basic concrete frame before the rains came, and as Table 3.1 shows this required a 90,000 taka payment to the mason. Oni had not sent enough, so she sought two loans, one from the MFI Grameen Bank and a more expensive one from a relative, to whom she paid 3 per cent a month in interest until remittances allowed her to repay it in full in November. There were also smaller loans taken from neighbours and family.

Figure 3.3 shows Panna's cashflow, aggregated to quarterly totals.

The remittances dominate the income side (there is virtually no other income), but flow in unevenly. Construction costs dominate the expenditure side and are also uneven. Bridging the gaps are loans and their repayments. Panna's ordinary expenditure is very modest: her median weekly outlay to look after her family of three was USD 55, less than

(Continued)

Panna's story: Continued

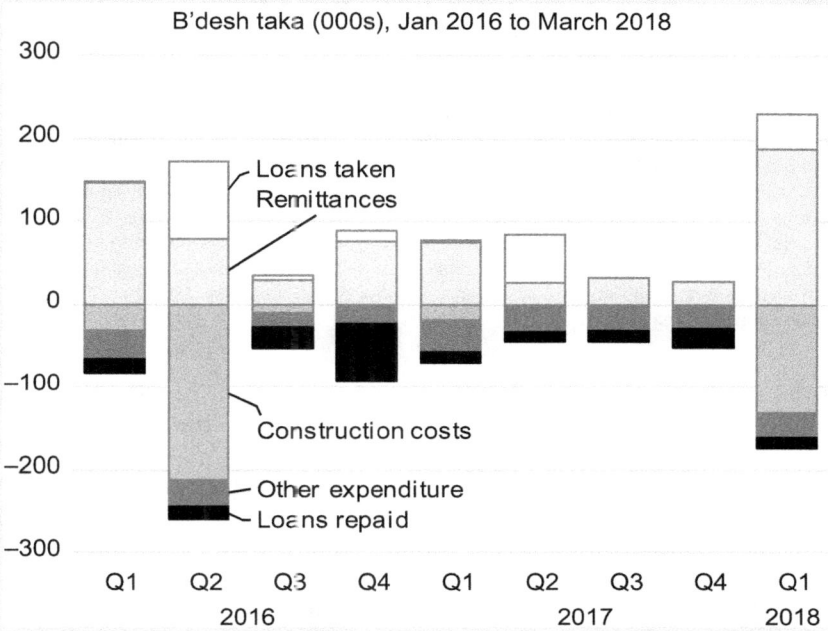

Figure 3.3 Panna's quarterly money flow

Photo 3.6 Panna's new home
Credit: Kalimullah

(Continued)

Panna's story: Continued

that of several much poorer diarists. Meanwhile, her construction costs average out at USD 117 a week; more than double her other expenditures and a testament to just how costly home improvements can be for poor families.

At this stage, in March 2018, the shell of the house was almost complete (Photo 3.6). Progress, though slow, had been made, and Panna had every reason to hope that the end would soon be in sight. But in April 2018, just as this case study was being written, Oni lost his Singapore job. He had long crossed the age limit for migrant labourers of his kind, but had fought to stay on. He hadn't warned Panna of the situation for fear of alarming her. But on 26 April he turned up at home with all his baggage and broke the news to his wife.

He hopes to take care of his family by getting back his old job as a salesman and remains determined to finish the new house. He can raise some money by selling what's left of his share of the inherited farmland, but will need more. How he gets that remains to be seen.

In the case of another Bangladeshi, Panna, the use of remittances shows that building a home is more than just bringing together land, materials, and money.

Panna's case shows that home building can be a complex process embedded in family and social behaviour and entangled in the personal histories of the builders. It is also a reminder that, as was seen in Nikhil's case, loans don't necessarily simply pay for the building work; they are often used as adjuncts to other major sources of funding. They can function as either bridging loans, providing short-term finance while the borrower is waiting for a remittance or other major source of money to arrive; or as refinancing loans, repaying other (perhaps more expensive) loans taken earlier on.

Social and economic aspects of home improvement

A home is not just a shelter. It is also the theatre in which a family plays out its private and social life. It can even be a place of business that brings revenue to the family. Many self-employed people rely on their home for their livelihood. This may mean using the home as a small production facility, as is the case with traditional cottage industries; or using part of the home as a small shop where goods bought wholesale in large quantities are divided up and sold retail at a profit. From a finance perspective, home improvements in these cases can be more directly linked to income. From a social perspective, the use of a home beyond shelter adds a dimension of public access and must be properly accounted for within the framework of the local culture. This is demonstrated in the case of Nisrine, whose home is also a place of business.[9]

A helping hand: The role of non-financial services

The microfinance institutions that serve clients like Nisrine in Lebanon or Bumak in Cambodia understand the social benefit of improved housing such as better health, education, self-confidence, and social status. Some lenders have

Nisrine's story: When your home is also your business

Photo 3.7 Nisrine
Credit: Habitat for Humanity

Nisrine, from Lebanon, is a self-employed hairdresser and make-up stylist. She shares the ground floor of her father's 40-year-old home in a declining area close to one of the biggest refugee camps in the country. Her brother and his wife live on the upper floor. Nisrine successfully sought housing loans from Al Majmoua to improve the building, driven in part by the need to preserve the family's social reputation.

Most of Nisrine's work is carried out in her clients' homes or by inviting them to her own home. This sets her apart from the cases presented so far, all of whom work outside the home. Like many self-employed people, Nisrine's home is also her work place, which adds urgency to keeping it in good repair. One imperative for Nisrine is to ensure she can invite clients into her home and still comply with Muslim cultural norms regarding the separation of the sexes in public spaces. To this end she created a second entrance, allowing female clients access to her workroom without being seen by any men that may be in the house. The improvements allow Nisrine and her clients to engage in beauty treatments without risk, thus enhancing their comfort and safety, and her business.

also seen the underlying importance of land ownership in securing sustainable gains for low-income communities, especially women. These stories highlight the non-financial aspect of housing microfinance. Non-financial services may be technical, such as providing building advice and plans, or advisory like budgeting for a home improvement and advice on how to hire a mason. Sometimes financial institutions themselves provide non-financial services, and sometimes these are provided by a third party: a private company, an NGO, or a government entity. The pioneering Bangladeshi MFI Grameen Bank is one of them, concerns a Grameen Bank customer.

Samita's is a success story. But her success depended on a fragile combination of good sense and good fortune. Marrying a man with no land of his own is generally thought of as a misfortune, but in her case it meant that she enjoyed the security of holding land in her own name. She was lucky that Grameen Bank came to her area, and luckier still that they decided to offer housing loans and that she was eligible to receive one.

Housing finance is not just a matter of suiting the finance to the building process, but also takes into account the social, personal, and communal situations in which the borrowers find themselves. Cooperative Tosepantomin in Mexico, like other self-help organizations, recognized the

Samita's story: Grameen housing

Samita (Photo 3.8) was born into a poor uneducated family that struggled to survive on a small patch of farmland. When her father died she was not yet married, and the question of her inheritance was settled by her brothers. The local custom in such cases was that the brothers would divide up the land among themselves and compensate their sisters for the loss of their shares by promising to look after them. But Samita's brothers generously took the view that if she had some land in her own name her marriage prospects would

Photo 3.8 Time to get some new bricks, Mum
Credit: Stuart Rutherford

(Continued)

Samita's story: Continued

improve. And so it proved. She married and had two sons. While she was bringing them up Grameen Bank opened a branch nearby, and Samita became an early and enthusiastic member of a Grameen borrowing group. A woman of very disciplined habits, and married to a man who brought in an adequate if not large income, she had no trouble repaying her Grameen loans and soon became a 'Centre Chief' – chairperson of the 40-strong group of women who came together to make weekly loan repayments.

Grameen started experimenting with finance for housing in the 1980s and by the mid-1990s loans were available in many of their branches, including Samita's. When Samita applied she got one quickly, for she was an ideal borrower in Grameen's eyes. She had a perfect loan repayment record and she wanted exactly what the programme was offering: a basic low-cost conversion of her existing mud-and-thatch hut into a corrugated metal-roofed structure supported by reinforced concrete columns. One of Grameen's conditions for granting a housing loan was that the land on which the house stood should be registered in the name of the woman borrower, to give her protection in the event she was widowed, divorced, or deserted. Most of the women in Samita's Centre were housewives living in homes standing on land owned by their husbands. These men were generally not willing to transfer landownership to their wives just for the sake of getting a Grameen housing loan. Samita, however, already owned her land. She was granted a 25,000 taka loan (worth about USD 1,500 at the time), to be repaid in weekly instalments over four years (though in the event she paid it off in two). The loan was given mostly in kind: she received reinforced columns made on site by masons appointed by Grameen, windows and doors, and corrugated metal for the roof. The couple chose to make the walls of traditional compacted mud, and to help with this she took another, 'ordinary' Grameen loan.

Then things went wrong for Samita. Her husband left her and took up with another woman in a nearby village. Fortunately, as anticipated by Grameen's rules, her land and her house were secure. The boys are now persuading their mother to replace the improved home, now about 20 years old, with a modern reinforced concrete one. Somewhat regretfully, she has agreed.

Marlon's story: Government transfers and private-sector advice

Marlon works as a consultant for the Ministry of the Environment in Ocotal, Nicaragua, while his wife has a job at the local supermarket. They have one child, a girl now eight years old. Although they are a good deal better off than the other households described in this chapter, their initial shelter strategy was not dissimilar in that they began to build a house from their own resources They secured a subsidized plot in a development set up by the local municipality, started building, and then took two loans.

The first, of just USD 170, came from Caruna, a government-run cooperative. Combining this with their savings enabled them to finish the basic rooms. To add a decent bathroom and toilet they realized they would need technical help. So they approached FUNDENUSE, a microfinance company, which lent them USD 1,800 and linked them with the local office of Habitat for Humanity. Habitat provided technical guidance on the installation of an on-site sewage tank, which was beyond the skills of the mason who had done most of the couple's building work. As a result, a high-quality finish was achieved using locally made adobe blocks, concrete walls, and zinc roofing for a shower and adjoining toilet. The couple have described the considerable impact the bathroom has had on their self-esteem and on their daughter, who now bathes each morning before she goes to school, having previously been too scared of the dark and the flies to visit the old toilet.

long-established practice in their rural community of neighbours helping neighbours build each other's homes, much as they help each other during planting or harvest. This system enables cash-poor communities to reduce the cost of home construction. The cooperative went a step further and formalized the practice as part of a framework that allowed the obligation to be treated as a financial asset. A member of the cooperative who provided his labour in the construction of his neighbour's home would be counted as having 'saved-up' the equivalent value of the construction labour. This served as the mandatory deposit needed to qualify for a government housing subsidy (e-MFP, 2017).

Such subsidies are an example of the key role governments play in housing in many countries. They also help build the enabling environment to encourage housing finance for the poor, as was seen in Chapter 2, and regulate and refinance lenders (Chapter 5). The final case in this chapter (Marlon's story), from Nicaragua, describes how a local government scheme for allocating unused land to poor households, plus access to subsidized financing, can get a family started in building their home. They were helped along the way with additional housing microfinance as well as non-financial technical advice that enabled housing that might otherwise have been out of reach.

Technical assistance like the advice that Marlon and his wife got from Habitat for Humanity will vary according to local norms and the availability of materials and skills. Similarly, recognition of communal building practices, as in the case of Tosepantomin, and social engineering, like Grameen Bank's insistence that the land on which loan-assisted housing is built is registered in the name of a woman, must naturally be adapted to the local context. Nevertheless, they illustrate the variety of ways that non-financial services can be added to financial services and thereby magnify the gains to the householder. This is an area of activity with scope for growth, and is discussed again in Chapter 4.

Notes

1. See <www.communityplanning.net/JohnTurnerArchive/pdfs/Freedomto BuildCh7.pdf>.
2. Adapted from Olivia Caldwell, Miyamoto International.
3. Names from unpublished case studies have been changed.
4. All stories from the financial diaries use dollars based on purchasing power parity (PPP), unless otherwise noted.
5. Adapted from Habitat for Humanity (2018)
6. Evidence from poor families shows that they don't generally use formal savings accounts to accumulate funds, but do use them for payments and remittances. Data from the World Bank's 2017 Global Findex survey shows that while 35 per cent of adults in low income countries had some type of account, only 11 per cent saved at a financial institution.
7. While many microfinance lenders require their members and borrowers to save, these savings are generally 'compulsory' while a loan is outstanding,

and serve to protect the lender against default. Some lenders, particularly for larger housing loans and micro-mortgages, do require a savings balance as a pre-requisite.

8. An informal system of money transfer.
9. Adapted from Habitat for Humanity (2018).

References

Daryl et al. (2009) *Portfolios of the Poor*, Princeton University Press, Princeton, NJ.

El Qorchi, M., Munzele Maimbo S. and Wilson, J. (2003) 'Informal Funds Transfer Systems: An Analysis of the Informal Hawala System', Occasional Paper 222, International Monetary Fund.

e-MFP (2017) 'Cooperativa Tosepantomin Mexico' in Report on the European Microfinance Award 2017: Microfinance for Housing, European Microfinance Platform, Luxembourg <www.e-mfp.eu/sites/default/files/resources/2018/01/European%20Microfinance%20Award%202017%20brochure_web.pdf>.

Habitat for Humanity (2017) 'Microsavings for Housing Finance' in Shelter Innovation Highlights, Terwilliger Center for Innovation in Shelter <www.habitat.org/sites/default/files/microsavings-for-housing-finance.pdf>.

Habitat for Humanity (2018) 'Household Profiles: Clients of MicroBuild Fund Investees' Habitat for Humanity's Terwilliger Center for Innovation in Shelter, Atlanta, GA.

Habitat for Humanity (2019) *How Social Norms Shape Low-Income Home Construction in Kenya - Consumer Insights and Systems Mapping*, Habitat for Humanity's Terwilliger Center for Innovation in Shelter, Atlanta, GA.

Rutherford S. and Sukhwinder A. (2009), *The Poor and Their Money*, Practical Action, Publishing, Rugby.

Rozas, D. (2016) 'Market growth: Loan sizes, remittances, and overindebtedness?', Cambodia Special Circular Dec 2016, MIMOSA.

Turner, J.F.C. (1972) 'Housing as a Verb', in J.F.C. Turner and R. Fichter (eds), *Freedom to Build, Dweller Control of the Housing Process*, pp. 148–175, Collier Macmillan, New York.

Author biography

Stuart Rutherford, who qualified and practised in the UK as an architect, is now an honorary senior fellow of the University of Manchester's Global Development Institute. He has written extensively about financial services for poor people, notably in *The Poor and Their Money* and in Collins et al. *Portfolios of the Poor.*

CHAPTER 4

Housing microfinance

Sandra Prieto and Patrick Kelley

What are the current trends in housing microfinance that should be considered by financial institutions when designing human-centred products and services that reach different market segments? This chapter describes global trends in housing microfinance demand and supply: the underserved low-income groups borrowing to improve their homes, and the financial institutions offering housing microfinance loans to them. It highlights the importance of the human-centred product development process for housing microfinance and presents what is known about the impact housing microfinance loans have on the lives of low-income people in the developing world. Toolkits and studies, developed by Habitat for Humanity's Terwilliger Center and used with dozens of financial institutions, present a comprehensive picture of housing microfinance today.

Keywords: housing; microfinance; affordable housing finance; microfinance institution; inclusive finance; product development; human-centred design

The stories of Nikhil, Panna, and other clients presented in the preceding chapter illustrate the human experience behind housing microfinance. This chapter aggregates those individual experiences to describe the demand side of housing microfinance and then goes on to present the supply side: the financial institutions offering housing microfinance loans to their clients. It closes with a discussion of housing microfinance product development and what is known about the impact of these loans on the lives of clients.

This chapter draws on the combined experiences of its authors of advising institutions in the design of housing microfinance products, and studies conducted by Habitat for Humanity with microfinance institutions and their customers. It draws heavily on the *State of Housing Microfinance* (Habitat for Humanity, 2017a) and *State of Investment in Affordable Housing* (Habitat for Humanity, 2017b) reports, and the *Housing Microfinance Handbook* (Habitat for Humanity, 2015); all produced by Habitat's Terwilliger Center for Innovation in Shelter (unless otherwise noted, all charts and figures in this chapter are sourced from these three publications; Habitat for Humanity, 2017a, 2017b, 2018). We begin with Habitat's own journey to become a leading voice in housing microfinance (Box 4.1).

http://dx.doi.org/10.3362/9781780447681.005

Box 4.1 Habitat for Humanity's journey to address affordable housing through microfinance

Lyndsay Taylor was living in a one-bedroom apartment with her three children in the United States. The conditions were poor, the neighbourhood unsafe, and there was not enough space for her family; but she could not afford to move. Then she heard about Habitat for Humanity's programme to help people like her build their own home. To qualify, Lyndsay first had to volunteer to help others in her neighbourhood build their homes. She also had to take classes in homeownership and save for a down payment, all while maintaining her job and supporting her family. Today, Lyndsay owns her home, built with help from other Habitat partners and volunteers, with enough space for her whole family and a mortgage she can afford.

Since 1976, Habitat for Humanity has helped people like Lyndsay own new, affordable houses with a focus on volunteers, community participation, and interest-free loans. This model has helped Habitat become one of the most respected non-profit organizations in the United States. Yet, this model alone is insufficient to address the shortage of affordable housing, estimated at 1.6 billion people worldwide. To meaningfully contribute to the world's massive quantitative and qualitative housing deficit, Habitat began working with financial institutions to develop and offer housing microfinance products and services.

Today, Habitat for Humanity has helped more than 80 financial institutions to develop and offer housing microfinance loans, focusing on market research, product development, and product performance monitoring, as well as impact and outcome evaluations of housing microfinance. In 2015, to further catalyse the market, Habitat published a housing microfinance handbook that remains a free resource for the design and rollout of locally adapted housing microfinance products. In 2016, Habitat for Humanity created the Terwilliger Center for Innovation in Shelter as a long-term commitment to its role as facilitator of private sector solutions to housing. The Terwilliger Center has a mandate beyond housing finance and housing microfinance solutions. It seeks systemic changes in the way the housing and construction markets serve low-income people, including materials, labour markets, transportation, and distribution, as well as financial services.

Demand: Housing microfinance clients

Fifteen years ago, little was known about microfinance clients accessing shelter finance. Today, research shows that as products have expanded, so too has the profile of housing microfinance clients, who now include not only informal income earners, but a broad range of customers excluded from formal financing for housing.

Microfinance institutions frequently segment the market by income, gender, and location for better targeting. Understanding the characteristics of different segments can promote a longer-term relationship with the financial institution, which reduces default risks and increases loyalty among clients. Additional products and services can also be provided to support customers through the incremental building process to achieve their 'dream home' in stages.

It is no surprise that income levels look very similar between housing microfinance and other microfinance clients; however, housing microfinance includes a wider range of repayment sources. Most financial institutions offer housing microfinance loans to serve their traditional customer base. Some,

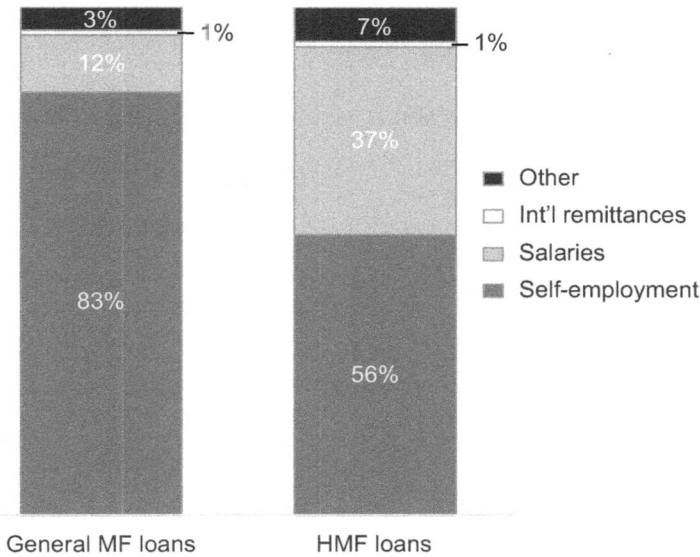

General MF loans   HMF loans

Figure 4.1 Source of repayment

however, use housing microfinance to segment or expand this base to include non-traditional clients with salaries (Figure 4.1). Civil servants such as teachers and police officers, and private sector factory and garment workers, are typical examples of low-income, salaried workers who face exclusion from traditional housing finance markets. The relatively stable income of this population segment is attractive to those financial institutions looking to offset the risk posed by self-employed borrowers and the longer tenors of housing microfinance loans. For others, such as Select Africa, this segment is their target market, as described in Box 4.2.

Women are another important market segment, and housing microfinance has fostered gender equality and empowerment of women. But intra-household decision-making also needs to be considered. Often, incremental

---

Box 4.2 Select Africa customer segmentation

Select Africa is a retail financial services group primarily dedicated to extending housing microfinance loans to unbanked public-sector employees in four countries of sub-Saharan Africa: Kenya, Malawi, Lesotho, and Swaziland. Select identified low-income civil employees as a stable, underserved market in 1999 and began lending to them. Loan repayments were secured through direct payroll deductions. After discovering that clients frequently used personal loans to finance housing, Select developed a product to support incremental housing construction which required larger sizes and longer tenors than their traditional loans. Select currently serves approximately 55,000 borrowers, with over 60% of its portfolio invested in housing (Habitat for Humanity, 2018a).

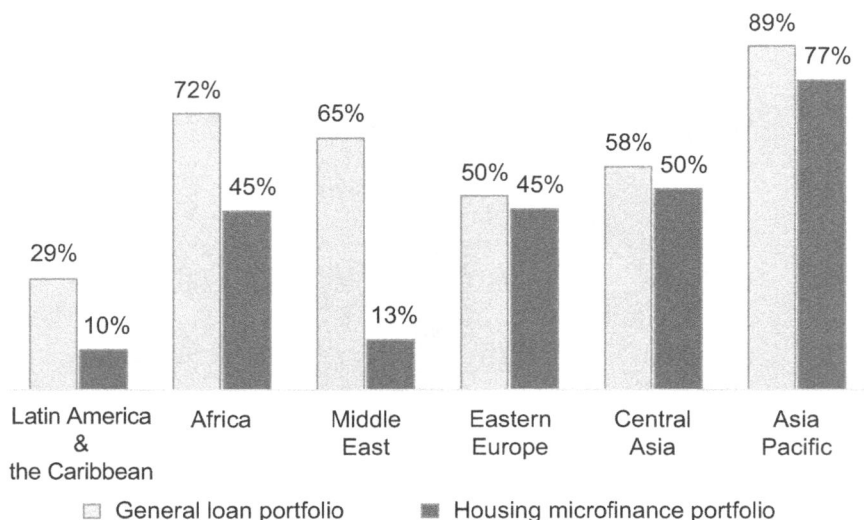

Figure 4.2 Average percentage of female borrowers

building decisions, and even the amount of money that can be set aside to repay a loan, are determined not solely by the borrower but with input from other household members. Today, women are more likely than men to take a microfinance loan, and this holds true for housing loans as well, although by a smaller margin. There are major regional differences as well: in Asia, nearly 80 per cent of housing microfinance borrowers are women, compared with less than 10 per cent in Latin America (Figure 4.2). Although these figures largely mirror the likelihood of a woman to take any microfinance loan, in the Middle East (and to a lesser extent in Africa and Latin America) there appears to be a cultural factor, as women are far less likely to take a housing loan than a standard microfinance loan.

In terms of location, housing microfinance loans are growing most in rural and peri-urban areas, although there are major regional differences. In Asia and the Pacific, rural clients comprise a very high percentage of housing microfinance portfolios. Africa, the Middle East, Eastern Europe, and Central Asia display a mix of rural and urban clients, while in Latin America and the Caribbean the market trends towards urban clients. As described in Chapter 3, while demand for affordable housing is strong in urban areas, and is expected to increase, urban housing microfinance can be challenging due to difficulty accessing land and the prevalence of renting over owning. However, opportunities do exist for housing microfinance and other housing loans for urban rental housing. High immigration rates (both economic migrants and those displaced from conflict areas) and proximity to markets present constant demand for affordable rental housing. This presents an opportunity to design housing microfinance products for small landlords (often themselves low-income households) to improve rental units serving low-income populations.

Supply: Providers of housing microfinance products and services

Microfinance non-governmental organizations (NGOs) or microfinance banks serving excluded populations were the first financial institutions to offer housing microfinance products and services. Today, a wider range of financial institutions has entered this arena (Figure 4.3). Thirty per cent of financial institutions offering housing microfinance loans are non-bank finance companies or institutions (NBFC/NBFI), with NGOs and microfinance banks comprising the second and third largest groups at about 20 per cent each. New entrants include dedicated housing finance banks and commercial banks, reflecting a trend to diversification of institution types offering housing microfinance loans.

As the number of financial institutions offering housing microfinance products grew (nearly doubling between 2006 and 2011), the availability of those products has likewise increased (see Figure 4.4).

Sixteen per cent of institutions surveyed added a housing microfinance product the same year the institution was founded, and 41 per cent within the first five years (Habitat for Humanity, 2017a: 13). These trends highlight the shift in perception of housing microfinance by financial institutions. Initially seen as a way to retain clients, or as a cross-subsidized product, housing microfinance has become a viable business proposition in its own right.

Large institutions diversifying into housing microfinance brings more capacity to finance shelter: 32 per cent of institutions responding to Habitat's 2017 State of Housing Microfinance report have assets in excess of USD 75 million while only 14 per cent have assets under USD 5 million.

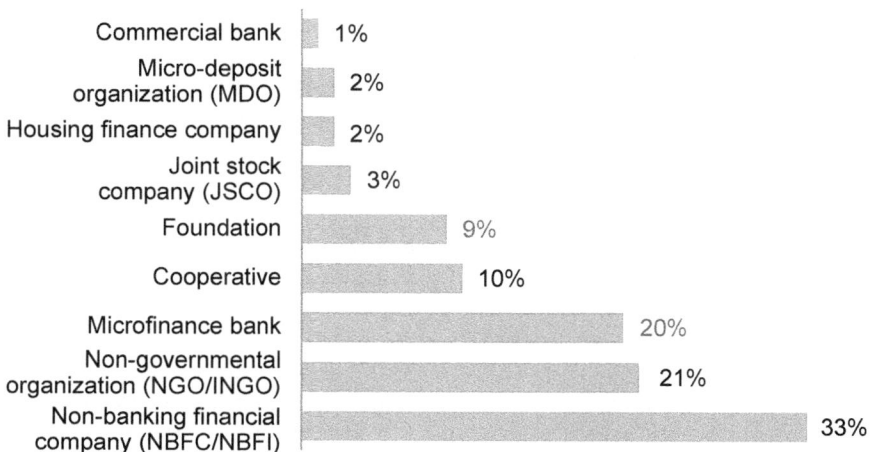

Figure 4.3 Institutions offering housing microfinance products[1]

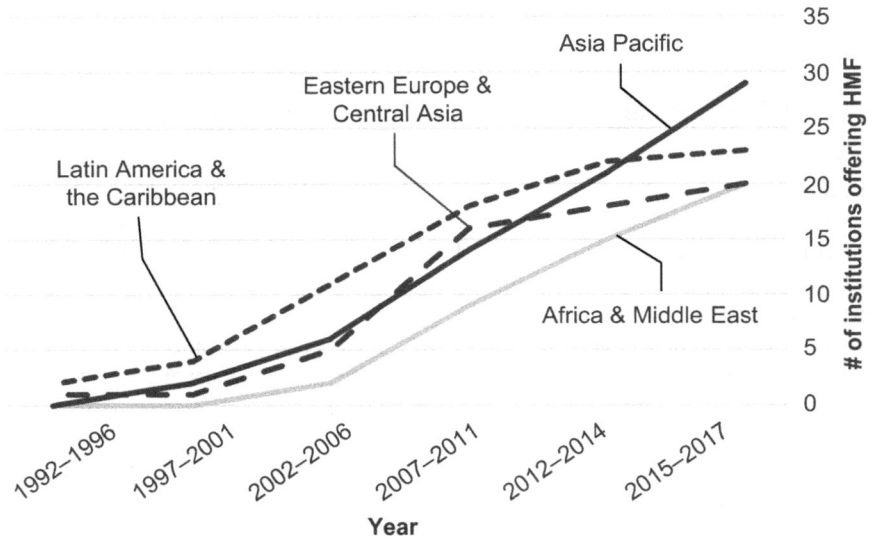

Figure 4.4 Introduction of HMF products

This is an important development given that housing lending is more capital intensive than short-term microfinance loans or consumer loans.

The shifting composition of financial institutions is not uniform across regions. In Africa, the most marked change has been the transformation of NGOs into microfinance banks. With increasing professionalism and stronger back-office support, these institutions have led the growth and expansion of the market. In Asia, government-driven initiatives have expanded the sector. India's 'Housing for all by 2022' programme described in Chapter 2, for example, includes a credit risk guarantee fund for low-income housing available to financial institutions beyond the traditional housing finance companies (HFCs) that once dominated housing lending (with a focus on middle- and upper-income borrowers). NBFCs and microfinance institutions (MFIs) can now provide unsecured housing loans to eligible borrowers, while a new breed of HFCs has built a new micro-mortgage market focused on the upper ranks of the urban poor who have until now been locked out of housing finance.

In Latin America and the Caribbean, microfinance banks and NBFC/NBFIs with deeper pockets are increasing their share of the market for housing microfinance, compared to the cooperatives that were more prevalent in the past. Mibanco in Peru (see Box 4.3) is a case in point.

Over time, the range of housing microfinance products and services has expanded from limited adaptation of traditional microenterprise loans to innovative housing loans, along with some savings and insurance products. Table 4.1 provides a comparison of traditional microenterprise and housing microfinance products, showing that they reach different market segments

---

Box 4.3 Mibanco

Mibanco is one of the largest housing microfinance providers globally. It is Peru's largest microfinance bank and one of the pioneers of housing microfinance in Latin America. Its *Micasa* (my house) loan product reaches over 201,000 clients and represents approximately 18 per cent of Mibanco's entire loan book as of May 2017. Operating within a highly mature and competitive microfinance market, Micasa has reached scale partly due to simple and fast loan processing. Mibanco's mission is to transform the lives of its clients through financial inclusion. Micasa is instrumental in fulfilling this mission because, as compared with other loan products, it directly impacts the household, benefiting the entire family and building client loyalty.

---

and target different stages of incremental building. Whereas traditional microenterprise loans are focused on the working capital needs of low-income households, housing microfinance products are focused on building an asset. The larger loan amounts of housing microfinance require longer loan tenors to align with the incremental building process and to keep payments affordable, considering the income levels of low-income borrowers. With both types of loans, the informal nature of many clients' incomes together with their lack of land title, make alternative forms of collateral necessary.

In 2018, 64 per cent of institutions reported that the housing microfinance portion of their portfolio was growing faster than their overall portfolio, while 30 per cent mentioned that it was growing at the same pace. Thus, while housing microfinance still represents a small part of microfinance portfolios, this is changing.

Housing microfinance products and services

As financial institutions expand the housing microfinance portion of their portfolios, products and services are evolving to reflect the diversity of customers and geographic locations. These changes can be seen in trends of loan use, size, tenor, and interest rate.

Table 4.1 Comparison of microenterprise and housing microfinance loans

	Microenterprise loan	Housing microfinance loan
Loan use	Working capital	Home improvements, repairs, and incremental construction
Population	Low-income households. Informal workers	Low-income households. Informal and salaried workers
Loan amount	Average between USD 300 and USD 1,000	Average between USD 1,000 and USD 3,000
Loan term	Between 3 and 12 months	Average is 32 months
Guarantee or collateral	Personal guarantees, moveable assets and inventory	Personal guarantees and informal proxy indicators of tenure security
Interest rate	Usually above 20%	Similar to microenterprise loans

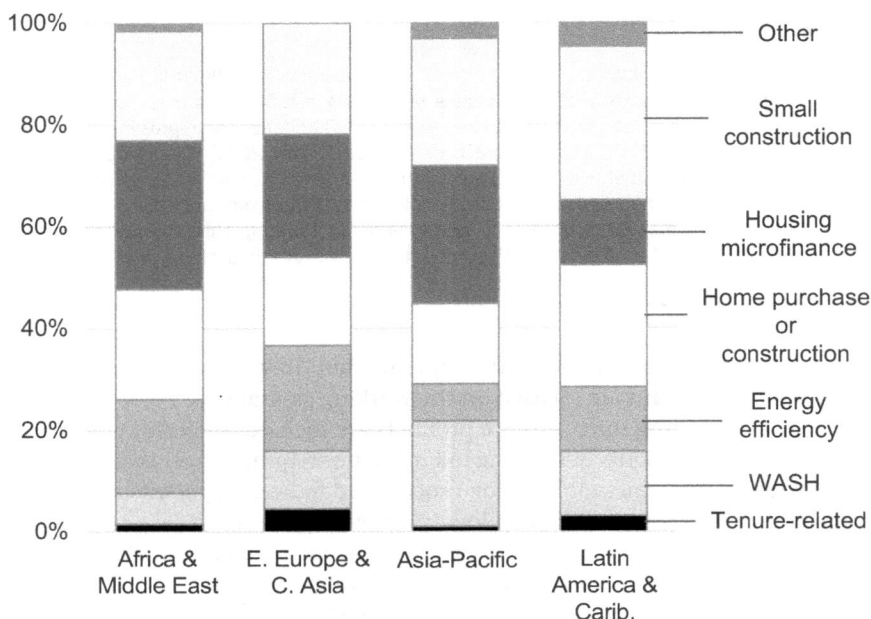

Figure 4.5 Commonly available HMF loans

Loan use

Most housing microfinance loans are used for small, incremental construction such as home improvement and expansion. In a small number of cases, housing microfinance loans are combined with other funding to allow for full house construction. But trends show that housing microfinance loans are now being used for needs beyond basic construction, such as the addition of latrines and solar panels (see Figure 4.5 and the WASH section in Chapter 2).

While demand for construction is spread evenly across all regions, these newer loan uses have a regional flavour. For example, water, sanitation, and hygiene (known collectively as WASH) loans have higher demand in Asia and the Pacific compared to other regions, while energy efficiency loans have higher demand in Eastern Europe and Central Asia. Financial institutions are revising their housing microfinance loans to accommodate these uses. For example, Koperasi Mitra Dhuafa (KOMIDA), one of the largest microfinance institutions in Indonesia, launched a WASH product in 2015 for the purchase of water filters, water pumps, and toilets. The maximum loan amount is USD 400 for a period of 6 to 24 months, and borrowers attend an orientation session on hygiene prior to disbursement. Seventy-five per cent of the loan is disbursed immediately for purchasing materials and labour, with the balance released on project completion. In the period from 2017 to 2019, almost 22,000 clients benefited from this facility for a total of USD 6.5 million in loans.

In another example, Kenya Women Microfinance Bank (KWFT) finances the purchase of rainwater catchment systems (including large tanks), water filters, energy-efficient cook stoves, and solar panels. Each of these is supplied by a vendor under agreement with KWFT. Such loans face minimal risk of fund diversion because no cash is disbursed – KWFT pays the vendor directly on behalf of the borrower. The direct connection between bank and vendor allows timely delivery, high-quality products, and good support services.

Some financial institutions are realizing that rental housing is an innovative product that allows borrowers to earn income from their property. Letshego Holdings Ltd launched a fairly standard housing microfinance product in Kenya in 2012, with loans up to USD 5,000 for 24 months. Growing urban populations and younger households' preference for renting increased demand for rental properties and Letshego became aware that many of its clients were using housing microfinance loans to invest in construction to serve this market. Letshego began lending to this sector and today offers loans from USD 10,000 to USD 25,000 for up to 72 months at 14 per cent flat interest, focusing on the urban centres of Nairobi and other up-and-coming cities of Kenya. Because housing finance entails larger loans and results in a higher-quality portfolio, profitability is solid. Moreover, financing for rental housing is an unexploited niche, where there's negligible competition and plenty of room to grow. Currently, just over 50 per cent of Letshego Kenya's loan portfolio is in housing (adapted from Habitat for Humanity, 2018a: 18).

Loan size

Housing microfinance loans tend to range between USD 1,000 and USD 3,000, with some regional variation (see Figure 4.6). Because the cost of making home improvements is high relative to other types of microfinance investments, housing microfinance loans are, on average, larger than working capital,

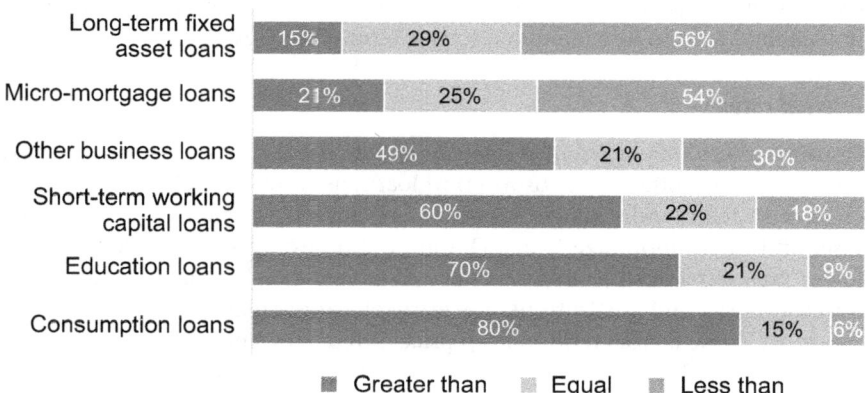

Figure 4.6 Average loan size: HMF loans vs. other microfinance products

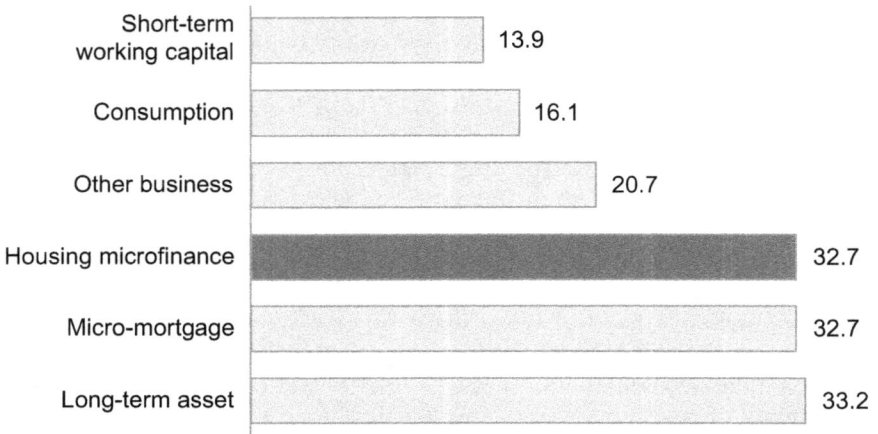

Figure 4.7 Average loan tenor (months)

education, other business, and consumption loans, although they are smaller than fixed assets and micro-mortgage loans.

In Latin America and Asia, institutions appear to be expanding into micro-mortgage lending, with housing microfinance loans greater than USD 15,000.

Loan tenor

Variation in loan tenor is another confirmation of the trend towards products designed to support specific housing needs. The average tenor of housing microfinance loans, based on global data, is 33 months (see Figure 4.7). This is about twice as long as consumption loans (16 months) and short-term working capital loans (14 months), and similar to micro-mortgage and long-term fixed-asset loans at an average of 33 months. Commercial mortgages, if available, tend to be for a much longer term (CAHF, 2019: 8).

Interest rates

Housing microfinance interest rates are either equal to, or lower than, short term working capital and consumption loans, as shown in Table 4.2.

As with loan tenors, lenders appear to be aligning interest rates with fixed asset and micro-mortgage loans. Despite the desire by some lenders to offer lower rates for housing, interest rate differences can lead to price arbitrage by customers, and institutions are wary of cannibalizing their other loan products. These factors tend to keep price differences small.

Lending methodologies, policies, practices, and delivery channels are also changing to reflect market demand and institutional preferences. Individual lending is the most common methodology for housing microfinance.

Table 4.2
loan products

	Short-term working capital	Long-term fixed asset	Other business loans	Consumption loans	Micro mortgage loans	Education loans
Greater than	10.7%	22.2%	14.5%	6.4%	18.8%	15.6%
Equal	39.3%	57.8%	45.5%	40.4%	65.6%	57.8%
Less than	50.0%	20.0%	40.0%	53.2%	15.6%	26.7%

This can have operational implications, especially where a different lending methodology is dominant for most of the loan portfolio. Modifications required when implementing housing microfinance products through an individual rather than a group lending methodology include changes to promotion, loan origination, loan use monitoring, and staff training.

However, some financial institutions with wide experience in group lending are applying it to housing microfinance loans as well. KWFT's Nyumba Smart Loan, a housing microfinance product offered through the same groups as other loans, has used group lending to keep costs low and repayments high. Lower loan origination costs over the life of the loan (18 months on average, compared to 12 months for standard microfinance loans) are also attractive. In other cases, a combination of lending methodologies is used to meet different needs, as described in the case of Microfund for Women in Box 4.4.

Loan underwriting policies

In addition to adaptation of lending methodology, there are some additional risks in housing that lenders mitigate in the underwriting process. Over 80 per cent of institutions rely on credit history as their first requirement and a co-signer or guarantor as their second, for both housing and non-housing loans. However, lenders may have additional requirements for housing loans

---

Box 4.4 Differentiation by product and lending methodology

Microfund for Women (MFW) is the largest MFI in Jordan with a market share of 35%. MFW currently serves more than 140,000 clients with a gross loan portfolio of over USD 90 million. MFW generally targets female entrepreneurs who require financing to start, expand, or improve their businesses, but recognizes housing as the second most requested product among its clients. In 2016, with support from Habitat's Terwilliger Center, MFW designed two housing microfinance products: a maintenance product, and a repair and renovation product. The former is offered through group and individual loans, which allows MFW to continue serving existing clients without collateral or guarantors. The latter is only offered through individual loans with collateral or a guarantor. Using both methodologies has allowed MFW to expand its outreach.

Source: MicroBuild Fund Quarterly report

related to income, title, or project. Some example of such additional requirements include:

- **Household income.** Underwriting policies must be adapted to allow for multiple sources of income if there are multiple earners living in the home.
- **Regular income.** Ninety per cent of housing microfinance lenders require customers to be able to demonstrate regular income (even if informal) and 58 per cent require at least one borrower to be a salaried worker.
- **Stable income.** In addition to verifying that income is sufficient, sources of income must also be sufficiently stable to accommodate longer tenors.
- **Land title.** Over half of all lenders require land title or land purchase agreement as collateral. Because acquiring title documentation can be a significant challenge for customers, some housing microfinance practitioners accept alternatives.[2] Table 4.3 shows an example from Uganda of the variety of accepted documents by several lenders for housing microfinance loans.
- **Project budget.** Lenders frequently require a written budget for the improvements being financed, as part of the loan application.

As with underwriting, the loan process for housing microfinance usually requires a few additional steps. In addition to the standard repayment capacity assessment, the proposed home improvement is assessed through reviewing an estimate of costs from a hardware store or other supplier (known as a Bill of Quantities, or BOQ), or a construction budget. Some lenders use this as an opportunity to engage the customers in a home improvement planning process to establish a relationship through a series of loans and other services that will allow the customer to complete their home incrementally.

If the loan has a non-financial component (see the section later in this chapter on non-financial housing support services), it is generally included in

Table 4.3 Land tenure documentation by branch

Bank Name	Branch	Title deed	Land sale agreement	Certificate of ownership	Land rate receipts	Letter from local authorities	Ancestral land
Centenary bank	Iganga	17%	70%			7%	7%
	Wakiso		90%		10%		
Opportunity bank	Jinja	18%	55%			27%	
	Kawempe	8%	83%	8%			
	Mubende		96%				4%
Pride Microfinance bank	Masaka		100%				
	Mukono	18%	76%	4%		2%	

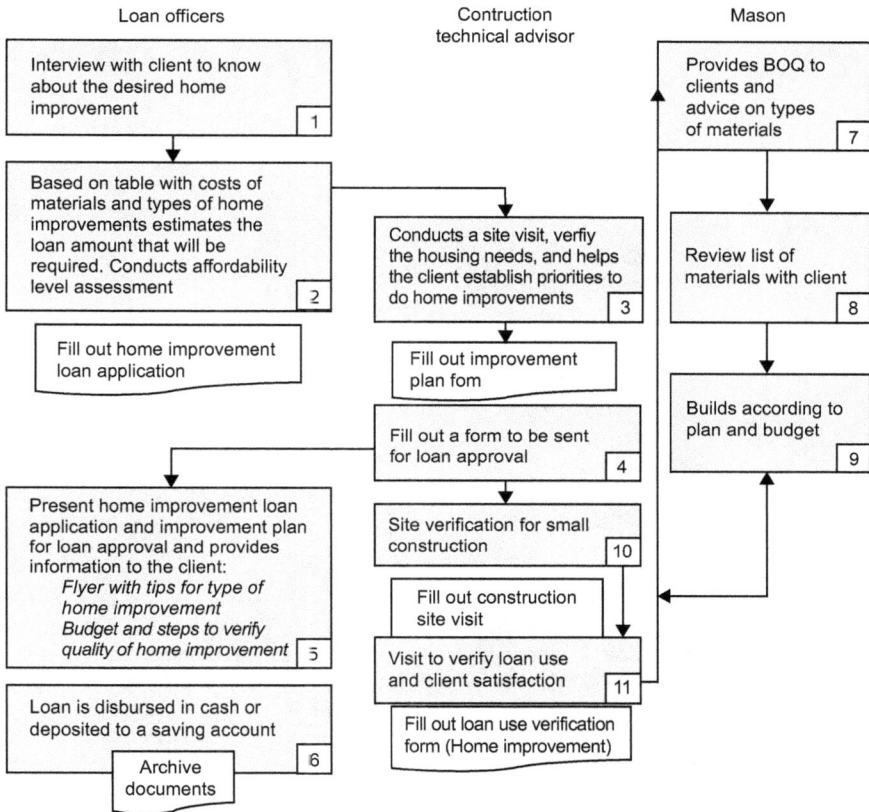

Figure 4.8 Sample loan process with housing support services

the loan origination process. The sample loan process in Figure 4.8 includes input from a construction technical advisor (who could either be on staff or an external advisor) as well as the mason doing the actual construction. Additional steps may include verification of loan use and on-site support for small construction. These activities help the customer at different points in the loan process, ensure completion of the home improvement, and reduce risk to the lender.

Home improvements can often run into delays or cost overruns. Therefore, in addition to verifying loan use, lenders monitor the home improvement itself. Figure 4.9 shows a variety of methods that can be used, but the most common form of loan verification is the site visit, followed by regular in-person meetings with borrowers. Where lenders have a light-touch approach to monitoring, adequate oversight of housing microfinance loans can be more burdensome. However, many lenders report that the operational requirements to monitor housing microfinance are no higher than those for other products.

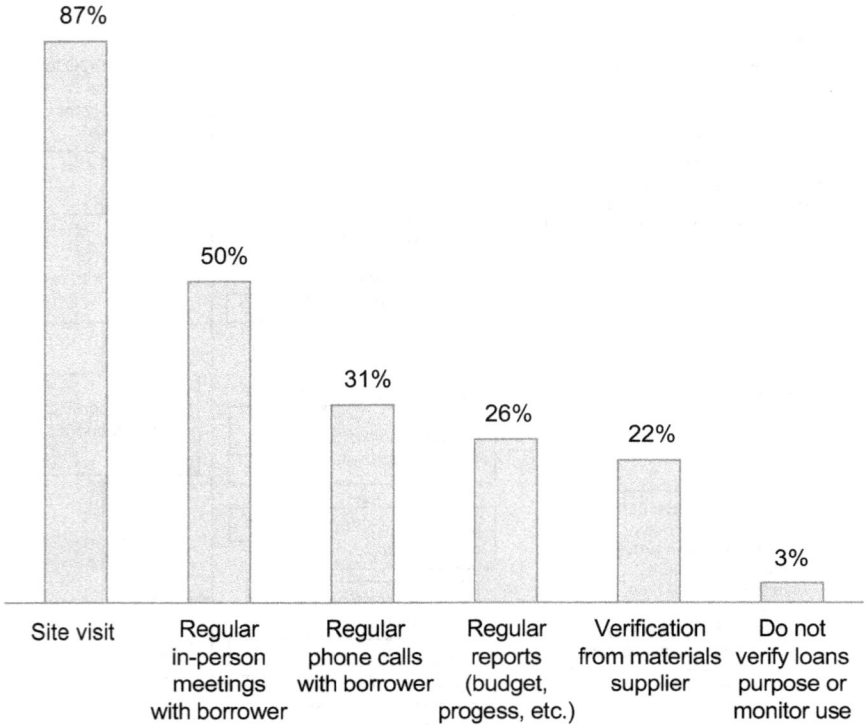

Figure 4.9 HMF monitoring practices

Delivery channels

Most lenders deliver housing microfinance products through their traditional branch offices. As alternative delivery channels such as agents, ATMs, smart cards, mobile phones, and the internet (including smartphone apps) are developed, these will also facilitate housing microfinance delivery. Such channels could be used to improve and reduce the cost of monitoring loan use and create links with other actors within the housing value chain, such as masons and building material providers. Two such examples of alternative delivery channels are currently being pilot tested: iBUILD® in Kenya and the Construapoyo card in Mexico.

iBUILD is a mobile and web-enabled platform that increases access to affordable housing in developing countries, using both basic mobile and smartphone technology. First launched in Kenya in 2019, iBUILD organizes the housing construction marketplace, allowing customers the ability to search for skilled professionals, solicit bids, purchase materials, and make payments through the app. Mobile payments can be made by bank, card, or mobile money account with easy cash out, and an escrow feature ties the release of funds to verified and geo-tagged milestone completions. Lenders can manage loan disbursements via iBUILD with full traceability of downstream transactions to contractors, workers, and material suppliers.

The Construapoyo prepaid card is another innovative delivery channel for housing microfinance loans. CEMEX is a producer and distributor of construction materials, with a worldwide presence. The company's Construapoyo card used in Mexico and Colombia allows borrowers to purchase building materials and receive advice to complete their home improvement. Shops affiliated with CEMEX allow cardholders to purchase materials with the same discounts offered to wholesalers. This approach has allowed financial institutions to offer a differentiated housing microfinance product, while reducing some delivery costs.

Housing microfinance: Achieving the double bottom line

For many financial institutions the main reason to offer housing microfinance continues to be the achievement of social impact. But responding to customer demand, reaching new market segments, and diversifying the loan portfolio are important reasons as well. Increasingly, housing microfinance products are being recognized as part of a strategy to expand into new market segments and create client loyalty, while simultaneously bolstering profits. Recent research confirms that housing microfinance has the potential to achieve these double bottom line results. However, as seen throughout this book, challenges remain to realize them. From regulation and policy constraints to capital shortages, these challenges will need to be overcome to unleash the full potential of housing microfinance to address the housing gap among low-income households, while allowing financial institutions to generate profits and reach scale.

Housing microfinance profitability

Smart institutions know that profitability comes partly from interest rate margins but also from new markets and lower operational expenses over the life of the product. While costs may be higher initially, the incremental building process can actually lead to lower costs over the life of an incremental building project. Forty per cent of clients take a subsequent housing microfinance loan immediately after repaying the first. If the financial institution has done its work up-front in the application and underwriting stages, it will have lower costs for subsequent home improvement loans. This is in addition to the fact that the loans are larger and longer term than standard microfinance loans, which also reduces marginal operating costs. Finally, profitability comes from cross-selling strategies. Financial institutions have more opportunities to sell additional products to clients who have a longer relationship through housing microfinance loans, and more opportunities to build client loyalty. Client loyalty, in turn, has the potential to reduce default risk and its associated costs. In theory, then, housing microfinance should strengthen the financial bottom line through lower operational costs and lower default risk over the life of the client relationship.

Practical experience bears this out. Overall profitability, based on interest revenue alone, tends to show housing microfinance being as profitable as other products offered by financial institutions – not very much higher or lower. Return on assets (ROA) for housing microfinance is often higher than ROA for general microfinance products (with some regional variation), and portfolio at risk (PAR) is generally lower.[3] While the profitability and ROA trends are self-reported and need additional empirical evidence to draw concrete conclusions, the PAR data has been confirmed through systematic collection of housing microfinance portfolio performance over a three year period. The global PAR of housing microfinance is reported to be around 4.6 per cent, compared to the PAR for overall microfinance portfolios at 5.4 per cent. Similarly, the average global write-off ratio for housing microfinance products is around 2.9 per cent; lower than the 3.45 per cent write-off ratio for general microfinance portfolios.

Determining the profitability of housing microfinance products requires analysis of funding costs, interest rate margins, delivery costs, quality of the loan portfolio, and risk premiums. Box 4.5 illustrates this type of profitability analysis conducted by KWFT.[4]

Box. 4.5 Can housing microfinance be profitable? The story of KWFT

The Nyumba Smart Loan ('Beautiful Home' in Swahili) was developed by KWFT to retain clients and attract new ones. KWFT hoped that profitability could lead to the growth of Nyumba Smart and its ongoing offering to clients. In 2017, Habitat for Humanity's Terwilliger Center for Innovation in Shelter and KWFT analysed the business case for the loan.

Cost of funds: Housing loans provided no real advantage on costs of funds, because there is no way to securitize loans and raise funds on the capital market. KWFT funds housing and business loans through a similar pool of sourced funds, often relying on overseas impact investors. KWFT's portfolio yield is around 28 per cent, with a funding ratio of 8.6 per cent, resulting in a net interest margin of 18.9 per cent.

Delivery/service cost: KWFT's operating expense ratio is about 22.4 per cent, and cost per borrower is USD 294. In 2016, the average loan size of KWFT's total portfolio was USD 914. The Nyumba Smart housing microfinance average loan size is only about USD 475. With a large focus on rural operations and smaller loan size, KWFT experiences high penetration costs; its cost-to-income ratio is very high at 96 per cent, partially mitigated by the group lending methodology. The housing loan is distributed similarly, and therefore has no advantage in the cost of lending.

Credit quality: Credit quality is where Nyumba Smart may have an advantage. As of December 2016, Nyumba Smart made up about 6 per cent of KWFT's overall gross loan portfolio and 11 per cent of the number of loans outstanding. Of the 11 products offered by KWFT, Nyumba Smart has shown outstanding performance with the lowest levels of portfolio arrears in terms of number of loans and value. Only 2 per cent of Nyumba Smart's portfolio was in arrears, compared with double digit arrears for some of KWFT's other products. As a result, KWFT considers Nyumba Smart the leading product among all the 'credit plus' products in terms of profitability. Primarily as a result of exceptional credit quality, therefore, Nyumba Smart has shown solid growth and has overtaken other products since its launch.

Social impact

The benefits of a better home are well known, and even small home improvements have been shown to have positive social impact (World Bank, 2007 & Habitat for Humanity, 2016). But these studies evaluate the impact of the improvement, not the finance that enables the improvement. Is there a difference?

Recent evaluations suggest that through housing microfinance, low-income households improve their housing conditions and, consequently, their quality of life. Non-financial benefits derived from housing improvements include reduction in illness based on a healthier environment, enhanced capacity for informal income earners to expand their businesses, and more stable environments leading to improved educational attainments in children.

LOK MCF, in Bosnia and Herzegovina, and ENLACE, in El Salvador, are two examples where these positive benefits were demonstrated. Evaluations showed that clients accessing housing microfinance loans were more confident coping with potential future disasters than a comparison group that hadn't yet had access to housing microfinance, and female borrowers exhibited high levels of empowerment.[5] An assessment in India revealed an increased sense of security and feelings of self-worth and pride as a result of housing microfinance.[6] These confirm that even small, incremental changes (such as improved roofing, improved walls, a separate kitchen, installation of flush toilets, or access to water through a piped connection) can lead to improved quality of life.

When discussing social impact, quality of information is a key concern. Fortunately, recent evaluations have used a rigorous, quasi-experimental design to maximize confidence in the results (Habitat for Humanity, 2018c).[7] While most results were positive, effects on health, wealth (financial and assets), and educational outcomes could not be measured during the period between baseline and endline data collection. This illustrates how use of a rigorous methodology can lead to more ambiguous results. It is particularly difficult to measure financial improvement outcomes when housing microfinance loan repayment could result in a temporary decrease in saving capacity. Over time these households may be in a better position to accumulate assets and wealth, as their improved living spaces will allow them to be more productive. In the same way, education outcomes were not measurable during the period of the research: while the environment for children to do homework was improved, the study duration was too short to show a measurable increase in performance at school, or improved career and salary, which could take years to materialize. Also, some of the indicators used to assess change in assets were not relevant to the whole sample. For example, refrigerators were used as one proxy indicator to measure assets. For those people who find fresh food daily and don't need a refrigerator, the indicator was not relevant. Qualitative evidence suggests there is more education and asset creation impact from housing microfinance, which underlines the importance of using mixed methodologies to assess impact.

Product
prototype
design

Market
research

Pilot
preparation
and
implementation

Product design and
market research
preparation

Institutional readiness
for housing microfinance
product design

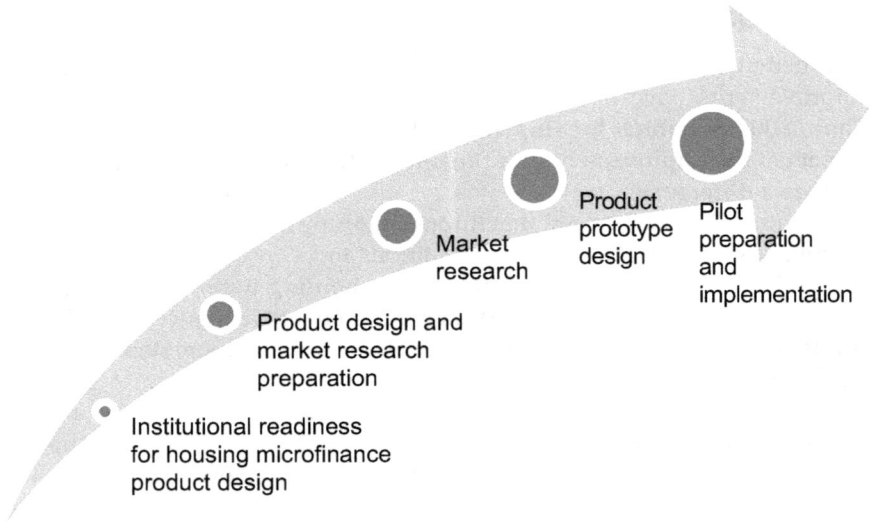

Figure 4.10 Five steps to develop housing microfinance products

The development of housing microfinance products and services

The product development process for housing microfinance products is similar to the process used to develop other microfinance products. However, financial institutions that have adopted a human-centred approach and have followed the five steps illustrated in Figure 4.10 to design their housing micro-finance products have succeeded at developing products that are relevant to the changing housing needs and priorities of customers, and streamlined institutional processes to improve operational efficiency and expand markets (Habitat for Humanity, 2015).

Successful institutions such as Mibanco and KWFT, described earlier, have undertaken housing microfinance product development with the following perspectives:

- **Approach product design comprehensively**, considering the housing-specific product features as well as delivery channels, marketing and positioning strategies, any added non-financial services (such as construction assistance), and customer satisfaction.
- **See housing as a process** so that products support incremental building until customers reach their end goal: a complete dream house.
- **Train front-line staff** with enough housing knowledge to make them capable of selling and promoting ownership of the product and positioning it as unique within the overall portfolio of products offered.
- **Monitor pilot implementation closely** to improve and prepare housing microfinance products for scale, including the level of capital required.

- **Look for opportunities to create linkages across the housing value chain** such as financial institutions, mobile network operators, builders, material suppliers and producers, and insurance companies.

Box 4.6 illustrates the approach by following the product development process of LOLC, one of the many financial institutions around the globe that have followed the stages mentioned above to design and/or refine their housing microfinance products.

Box 4.6 LOLC's journey to design a human-centred housing microfinance finance product and services[8]

Lanka Orix Leasing Company Cambodia, Plc (LOLC), formerly known as TPC, is one of the four largest MFIs in Cambodia, providing financial products and services to the underserved low-income market since 1994. In 2012, LOLC launched a loan product for home improvement. A year after its launch, the loan was offered in 11 branches, serving 549 clients with a portfolio valued at USD 1 million, and by early 2015 had grown to USD 5.9 million and 2,530 housing clients (Step I).

In May 2015, LOLC borrowed USD 2 million from Habitat's MicroBuild Fund to expand its housing portfolio (see Chapter 5 for an explanation of the MicroBuild Fund). Habitat's Terwilliger Center provided LOLC with technical support to refine the product and associated processes. LOLC started by conducting a customer satisfaction survey to understand satisfaction with the product features and delivery, including the provision of non-financial support services (Step II). Based on findings from the survey, LOLC identified the opportunity to increase the loan amount and loan tenor to reach out to new market segments (Step III). They increased the loan amounts up to USD 15,000 and extended the loan term up to 60 months (Step IV). In addition, LOLC developed a comprehensive strategy for expanding its housing portfolio, which included expansion to new geographic areas and bundling of housing microfinance with other financial products as part of a cross-selling strategy (Step V).

To achieve these goals, LOLC created new staff positions, including a housing product champion role, to help ensure long-term sustainability through close monitoring of product performance. The product champion role is relatively uncommon in the microfinance sector, but with a future-looking mandate, the product champion assisted LOLC's operational teams to recognize market opportunities and implement product refinements to capture these opportunities. LOLC also added a civil engineering specialist to assist clients accessing larger loans for construction rather than small home improvements.

Loan officers were trained on basic building technology and construction cost estimation, allowing them to more effectively assess the loan amounts needed by clients and train other staff as demand increased. Specialized loan officers were placed in branches with particularly high demand.

Once institutional capacity was in place, LOLC turned its focus to consumer education. Brochures with sample housing designs, quality indicators, and explanations of tools to enhance the quality of constructions were used to guide clients through the decision-making process as they considered their desired home and the incremental construction projects necessary to achieve that goal. These materials simplified discussing technical elements of housing quality and helped build customer loyalty. Finally, LOLC designed a communication strategy for promotion, positioning, and effective service.

Non-financial housing support services

As this chapter has shown, introducing housing microfinance products and services is a strategic choice. One consideration particularly relevant for housing microfinance is the addition of non-financial support services to help low-income households successfully manage the incremental building process. Incremental housing and the housing microfinance that enables it are not without risks. Chief among those risks is the concern that the self-build process common among low-income households around the world may lead to substandard housing outcomes. For that reason, the question of whether technical construction assistance should be offered as part of a housing microfinance product persists. Financial institutions that choose to do so have to determine what types of non-financial support services to offer, their costs, the service delivery model(s), and how these services will add value to clients.

In the context of housing microfinance, housing support services can generally be defined as the non-financial services that may complement a housing microfinance loan. There are many variations but all aim to put the borrower in a position of being able to maximize their housing results. Housing support services intend to improve a homeowner's incremental housing outcomes, reduce costs or wastage, and help a homeowner with associated services such as land documentation or to gain access to basic services. They can manifest as training, legal support, tips on the use of new materials or methods, assistance with hiring of technicians, direct services and advice, financial education, and incremental housing planning (see Table 4.4 for a description of different types of housing support services). Housing support services do not need to specifically focus on home construction: financial planning for a multi-step home improvement and land tenure rights assistance are two examples of services that would be considered housing support services but have sometimes been overlooked when thinking narrowly in terms of construction assistance.

Habitat for Humanity has invested considerable effort over the years exploring how to deliver housing support services sustainably and whether they improve good housing outcomes. This section draws on these efforts and references the 2017 State of the Sector Survey (Habitat for Humanity, 2017a), as well as findings from two internal Terwilliger Center studies.

Many financial institutions have ambitious plans for providing housing support services when designing a housing microfinance product. Their motivations are clear: they hold the social components to their mission deeply and have organizational cultures that centre on a concern for their clients' well-being. And it is true that badly built or located housing can lead to grave outcomes. The 2010 earthquakes in Haiti revealed how poorly engineered roofs in self-built homes collapsed, leading to injuries and deaths. In that light, attempting to design a package of services that help and protect clients in the housing process is natural. In fact, nearly half of all institutions responding to a 2017 survey offer housing support services in some form.

Table 4.4 Types of housing support services offered

Level of HSS	Key characteristics	Examples
Pre-prepared information – materials that address the most common challenges and opportunities faced by an identified segment of clients an institution is targeting.	**Brochures and pamphlets** – often short documents that deal briefly with one subject and that serve the dual purpose of promoting the housing microfinance product. For example, a brochure with tips on how to properly plaster a wall. **Technical sheets** – also about one specific topic, but more technical in nature and dealing with a specific aspect of housing or construction. For example, 'Documenting Your Land Rights'. **Construction guides** – a more detailed description of proper house construction and related technical aspects of housing, often in the format of a book.	Information kits; list of recommended builders and suppliers; referrals to MFIs; financial education; construction technical brochures, construction manuals, and videos.
Pre-construction advice and services – customized services tailored to the specific needs and situation of a particular client before the start of a project.	**Client construction** – discussion with clients about their desires, demands, and needs for their house, both in the immediate term and in the long term. Advice can be provided on ways to maximize client goals. **Develop plans** – there are two types of plans: a house plan for construction work to be performed with the first loan, and a master plan that maps out the total incremental building process that may entail multiple loan cycles to reach completion. Cost estimations, and assistance with permitting and titling are part of planning.	Design advice or services; assistance with permits; secure tenure legal support; builder training; assistance with estimation, materials, and labour scheduling; recommendations on materials and techniques; inspection of works.
Construction assistance – on-site advice and support to help maximize quality and outcomes.	**Advice and services** – related to a specific construction project involving one or more sites. Requires advanced construction skills. Typically associated with repairs, extensive maintenance, more complex home improvements, substantial renovations and extensions, and building new homes. **Basic, non-structural, and structural work** – Review of home improvement, repairs, or installation of utilities. Generally consists of advice, quality control, quality inspections, structural design, and disaster risk mitigation.	Non-structural works such as non-load-bearing masonry, bricklaying or carpentry; electrical and plumbing works; non-structural roofing. Structural work such as load-bearing masonry, bricklaying or carpentry; structural roofing; earthquake or other disaster mitigation.

Another reason institutions provide housing support services is to mitigate risk. Collapsing structures, cost overruns, or unscrupulous builders are some of the many ways that a housing project could lead to financial difficulties and, foreseeably, unpaid loans. The potential reduction of credit risk is an incentive for institutions to provide housing support services. The 'softer' housing support services (such as assistance in home renovation planning, budgeting, and selection of institutions) often focus on manageable execution risks to increase the likelihood of project success.

A third, but important, reason institutions provide housing support services is commercial. Housing support services can be a strategy to market and sell housing loans and to differentiate a product or institution in the market. This has become increasingly important as markets become more competitive in the microfinance sector, with more institutions vying for the same clients. Housing support services can help an institution and its products stand out among potential borrowers. Almost all forms of housing support services mentioned here provide an element of visibility and positioning in target communities.

An example of the subtle but powerful sales function of housing support services can be seen in Tajikistan, where the financial institution Arvand has hired and trained housing technicians in their branch offices. Customers coming into the branch for transactional purposes find a construction professional to talk to about their home renovation plans. Arvand finds that the construction professional is able to provide both planning insights and construction advice. In addition, the opportunity of meeting with a technician encourages some clients to begin a project that may have been stuck in procrastination.

Despite the social, client protection, and promotional reasons for providing housing support services, there is almost no reliable statistical evidence that proves its effectiveness. Evaluations have been inconclusive or lack statistically significant results of impacts on homeowners' outcomes. This holds true when measured in construction cost savings or housing quality outcomes. It may be that there are benefits occurring to households, but it has not been shown empirically. This lack of data is a challenge to cost-conscious institutions struggling to justify the additional staff or effort required to provide these services.

A reason cited by financial institutions for not providing housing support services is the fear of institutional liability for bad outcomes. If an institution recommends a certain type of material or a specific builder, a customer who is unhappy with the outcome of their project could refuse to pay back their loan. There is little evidence of this being a real problem or having caused significant credit risk leading to loan defaults. However, the fear factor is real. Most institutions that provide housing support services make disclaimers or have specific limits on their liabilities to mitigate this concern. In other cases, financial institutions avoid housing support services altogether.

The largest inhibitor to providing housing support services, however, remains the cost of providing or managing the delivery of services outside

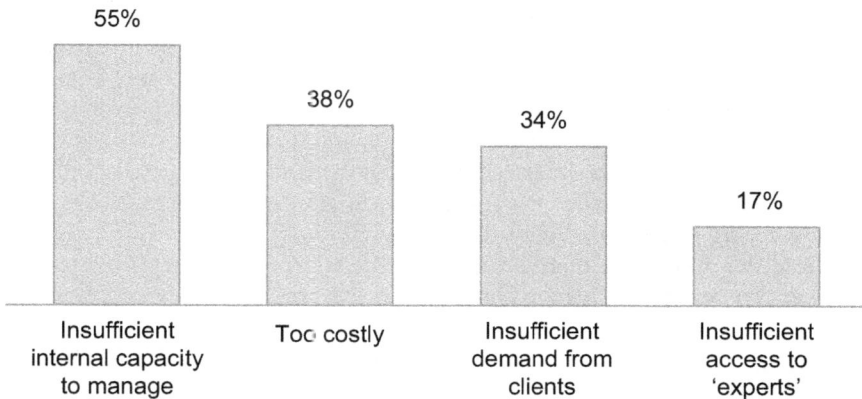

Figure 4.11 Reasons for not providing technical assistance to clients (% of institutions responding)

the financial institution's core competencies. There are limits to the number of things any one organization can do well, and some providers of housing microfinance decide to avoid taking on this service.

Figure 4.11 shows that 55 per cent of financial institutions cite lack of internal capacity as the reason they don't offer clients technical support and advice, while 38 per cent cite cost and 34 per cent point to insufficient demand from clients. The following section describes some of the delivery methodologies institutions have successfully used to address these constraints, as well as their limitations.

Considerations for delivery of housing support services

Almost as important as the type of housing support service is the way it is delivered to clients. There are three general models used by financial institutions to provide housing support services: Loan processing, technician services, and market linkages.

1. Loan processing

Loan processing builds on the channels used by a financial institution to interface with their customers, primarily the loan officer. Microfinance loan officers are well trained in financial assessments, so these housing support services tend to consist of basic financial planning for a home improvement, evaluation of project budget/borrowing capacity, or estimation services on project costs. Services are usually standardized, and staff can be prepared with some basic training and tools, but deeply technical content outside their capacity and expertise cannot be provided. For example, Kasagana-Ka Development Center, Inc. (KDCI) in the Philippines equips loan officers with a cost estimation tool to ensure that the loan amount granted is adequate to complete the project, avoiding both underfinancing and excessive funds that could be diverted for non-housing purposes. KDCI believes it can increase loan officer competency to deliver these services over time and that, eventually, they will be able to advise clients on how much a specific improvement will cost. They also foresee loan officers assisting in planning housing improvement on an incremental basis to align with client repayment capacity.

Because housing support services delivered within the loan process remains close to the core competencies of a lending institution, they can be low-cost while offering value to the institution.

Customer information and insight gathered through the provision of services can be used for loan evaluation and risk assessment. Indeed, housing support services delivered through loan process channels have been the most lasting and sustainable. The main critique of delivering housing support services this way is that their standardized, off-site approach may not be meaningful enough to impact housing quality.

2. Technician services

Qualified technician services bring specialized expertise to assist a client with their home construction or improvement project. The qualified technician may be on staff at the financial institution, but in many cases financial institutions have sought partnerships with a third party to provide these technical services. These partnerships are often with not-for-profit institutions such as local affiliates of Habitat for Humanity, PRODEL, and Build Change, which share a similar social mission with the microfinance institution and for whom partnership is mutually beneficial. Qualified technician services can sometimes be designed to be rigorous and with multiple visits to construction sites over the project cycle.

Alternatively, they can be designed with a lighter touch and lower cost, such as placing an advisor in a large branch to sit with applicants and evaluate their projects. Because qualified technician delivery is an additional cost to the institution, some have developed fee schedules or interest rate adjustments to pay for these services, or only provide them when clients opt-in. For example, ADEMI, a financial institution in the Dominican Republic, offers clients the option of on-site technician services through a partnership with Habitat for Humanity. There is a 3 per cent charge on the value of the loan for the service. Less than a quarter of ADEMI's estimated 400 housing clients a month opt-in to receive this advice.

These high-touch services are often perceived as providing the most substantial value to clients and to be the most impactful on housing quality. Anecdotal evidence of a technician's value is abundant, and technicians can point to numerous errors they were able to prevent clients from making. As mentioned above though, it has been difficult to find empirical evidence of systemic changes in housing quality resulting from qualified technician services. This becomes a substantial burden when considering their cost. This was the case for Hattha Kaksekar Limited (HKL), a microfinance institution in Cambodia. Its rapidly growing housing product surpassed 10,000 housing loans. However, it closed down a programme to offer housing support services from qualified technicians after clients reported that they didn't value advice from young trained technicians, preferring their trusted local mason instead.

3. Market linkages
Another approach to bringing industry specific expertise to housing support services is the market linkages approach, whereby private sector companies provide their products and services to an emerging lower-income class that is growing in market influence. Market linkage strategies build alliances with local construction businesses that provide technical advice as well as favourable pricing or delivery arrangements. The ability to promote their products or services can reduce or eliminate the costs of providing services through qualified technicians.

LafargeHolcim, the global cement company, has found that when providing technical assistance to housing microfinance borrowers, its turnover increased in the retail stores where those microloans are spent. Households benefit from quality construction inputs, reduced costs, and improved quality of home construction and improvement activities financed through a loan. In Indonesia and Nigeria, these programmes have reached substantial scale, providing housing support services to over 20,000 housing microfinance borrowers. In fact, their housing support service has grown beyond just those taking housing microfinance to reach 150,000 families. In Peru, MiBanco's MiCasa clients have the option to use their financing as a line of credit with one of two construction materials providers: HatunSol and Dino. HatunSol in turn provides delivery and some favourable pricing to clients. The partnership currently generates over USD 5 million in sales for HatunSol, and over 16 per cent of MiCasa clients have opted in.

Market linkages seem to offer the most promise for sustainability. However, like trying to provide qualified technician services, there have been many failures. The heavy logistics of an overwrought partnership have burdened some with frustrations and cancellation. It is important for businesses to enter with a firm conviction and intent to expand their market to low-income households. That conviction will help the company endure the steep learning curve and many iterations before getting it right.

The question of whether to provide housing support services remains a challenging question to any financial institution considering housing microfinance. Social motivations incentivize institutions to try, and with almost half of all housing microfinance providers offering them, there are benefits to doing so. However, evidence from practice suggests that institutions should be cautious. Starting slowly and adding complexity after success with simpler services close to existing core competencies seems to be a successful approach. Qualified technician services can make sense if an institution sees value in marketing and sales of the product. They are hard to sustain and pay for if only seen as a way to ensure construction compliance. The same lessons apply to linkages with the private sector. Social motivations alone are insufficient if either party faces complexities that their operations cannot sustain. A lesson from LafargeHolcim is that larger construction players can look beyond a particular partnership to the wider low-income market. Their ability to create large-scale systemic change in the housing and construction sector leads to benefits far beyond one or two partnerships with financial institutions.

Summary

Financial institutions serving the poor have long understood the high demand for housing loans among their clients. Today, housing micro-finance products are poised to become mainstream with greater market information about the clients that use housing microfinance, and the institutional adaptation required to successfully offer them. Done well, housing microfinance can support a double bottom line approach: products can diversify a financial institution's product offering with longer, larger loans without additional risk, while benefiting clients through improved health, business, and education. Best practices for institutions developing a housing microfinance product include:

- **Use a multi-disciplinary team** and invite other key actors who can contribute significantly to the prototype design.
- **Include the participation of field staff** that will be responsible for implementing the product, ideally field staff from the branch offices where the product will be piloted.
- **Think outside the box** when it comes to the non-negotiable attributes of the product. Keep in mind 'the healthy tension' between customer needs on the one hand, and institutional needs and capacity on the other; as well as the added value of establishing a competitive advantage.
- **Include all the costs associated** with the prototype: application, underwriting, origination, servicing, and monitoring, including any non-financial services. Establish an interest rate that is appropriate for the services provided. Customers are not choosing only based on price.
- **Consider loan officer incentives** that encourage promotion of the new housing microfinance product and set a monthly goal for loan officers who manage a multi-product portfolio.
- **Design-in measures to prohibit use of the loan for purposes other than for housing** such as reverting to the maximum interest in case of misuse of loan proceeds.
- **Consider if the prototype may cannibalize other products.** The product cannot exist in isolation and therefore cannot be developed without considering its impact on existing products. Insufficient differentiation among products can lead to inappropriate internal competition.
- **Evaluate the competition** and establish the product's competitive advantage. Review housing microfinance products on the market and other fixed asset loans that could be used by customers for housing.

- **Define and monitor customer satisfaction and financial and social performance outcomes** that can support product differentiation, improved customer experience, delivery channels, competitive advantage in the market, and improved lives through improved homes.

Notes

1. The survey data is self-reported and the publisher (Habitat for Humanity and its Terwilliger Center) has historical ties with financial institutions with a strong social mission. Commercial players may be less responsive or less likely to receive the survey; results may therefore under-represent commercial providers offering housing microfinance.
2. Alternative title documents may include land purchase agreements, inheritance documents, registration certificates, municipal use documents or cadastral plot certificates. Informal proxies may be utility or other bills, tax payment records, or references from neighbourhoods or local/communal authorities Some financial institutions may require more formal documentation for loans above a certain size; and some financial institutions are even partnering with local authorities to extend loans towards improving documentation of tenure. Though tenure security has been perceived as a barrier to the scalability of housing microfinance, current practice shows that despite the challenges, financial institutions are finding flexible alternatives to overcome them.
3. Here PAR refers to portfolio at risk at 30 days
4. Conversion rate at USD 1 = KES 103
5. Research implemented with the technical support of Oxfam Novib in 2015.
6. Study of housing microfinance clients of ESAF Microfinance and Investments Pvt Ltd (EMFIL) and Growing Opportunity Finance (India) Private Ltd (GOF).
7. Research conducted by Genesis Analytics and the Leibniz Institute for Economic Research. For example, a recent impact evaluation of 1,252 KWFT Nyumba Smart housing microfinance loan clients used a difference-in-differences method to compare outcomes in the treatment group at baseline and endline.These results were then compared with outcomes over the same period by a preselected control group. Because of concerns over statistical significance between certain indicators, the analysis used propensity score matching to improve the evaluation design. The selection of treatment and control sample sites was not random – comparable branches were selected.
8. Source: Habitat's Terwilliger Center-Case studies MicroBuild Investees (Angelo Naidas and Naeem Razwani), 2017.

References

CAHF (2019) *10th Anniversary Edition Housing Finance in Africa: A Review of Africa's Housing Finance Markets*, Centre for Affordable Housing Finance, Johannesburg, p. 8.

Habitat for Humanity (2015) *Microfinance Product Development: A Handbook, 3rd Edition*, Terwilliger Center for Innovation in Shelter, Habitat for Humanity, Atlanta.

Habitat for Humanity (2016) *Beneficial Impacts of Homeownership: A Research Summary*, Habitat for Humanity, Atlanta <www.habitatbuilds.com/wp-content/uploads/2016/04/Benefits-of-Homeownership-Research-Summary.pdf>.

Habitat for Humanity (2017a) *The 2016–2017 State of Housing Microfinance: Understanding the Business Case for Housing Microfinance*, Terwilliger Center for Innovation in Shelter, Habitat for Humanity, Atlanta.

Habitat for Humanity (2017b) *State of Investment in Affordable Housing*, Terwilliger Center for Innovation in Shelter, Habitat for Humanity, Atlanta.

Habitat for Humanity (2018a) *Building the Business Case for Housing Microfinance (in Sub Saharan Africa)*, Terwilliger Center for Innovation in Shelter, Habitat for Humanity, Atlanta.

Habitat for Humanity (2018b) *Household Profiles: Clients of MicroBuild Fund Investees*, Terwilliger Center for Innovation in Shelter, Habitat for Humanity, Atlanta.

Habitat for Humanity (2018c) 'Building Assets, Unlocking Access project- KWFT Housing Microfinance Product Impact Evaluation report', June 2018.

World Bank (2007) *Housing, Health and Happiness*, World Bank Policy Research Working Paper 4214, April 2007 <https://pdfs.semanticscholar.org/83b3/863e74db8260390e4cfeed32fdd1a9e213ba.pdf>

Author biographies

Sandra Prieto is an independent consultant. She spearheaded the launch of Habitat for Humanity's Terwilliger Center for Innovation in Shelter, and led the advisory services practice 2012–2018, to aid financial institutions to develop housing microfinance products. She is a seasoned consultant, speaker, and trainer, and has co-authored publications, on this topic, including the flagship publication *The State of Housing Microfinance* (2017), the only industry survey focused exclusively on the global growth and implementation of housing microfinance.

Patrick Kelley leads Habitat for Humanity International's Terwilliger Center for Innovation in Shelter. The Terwilliger Center seeks to strengthen affordable housing value chains, to stimulate innovation and enterprise solutions for shelter, and to mobilize investment capital to move housing solutions to scale.

CHAPTER 5

The funding landscape for affordable housing finance

Deborah Burand, Claudia Rojas, R.V. Verma, W. Britt Gwinner, Lucie Astier Such, Vinod Kothari, and Mona Kachhwaha

How can we increase flows of capital into housing microfinance? This chapter argues that the strategy for attracting more investments into housing microfinance should stand on at least three legs. First, the financial returns and risks of financing housing microfinance need to be better documented and shared with investors. Second, the positive social and environmental impacts from adequate, affordable housing need to be rigorously measured, analysed, and publicized. And third, risk mitigants and credit enhancements need to be tapped to ensure that capital flowing into housing microfinance carries financial terms that are commensurate with the risks. Acknowledging non-financial support will be needed in many markets to build a healthy ecosystem, institutional capacity, and a strong investment pipeline. This chapter presents concrete examples of steps being taken around the globe to increase funding for institutions that provide housing finance to those seeking to acquire or improve their homes. It describes new financial products, creative transaction structures, and the catalytic roles being played by private, public, and philanthropic funders to increase capital flows into housing finance in emerging markets.

Keywords: housing microfinance; risk mitigants; credit enhancements; catalytic capital; impact investors; social impact

Introduction

Deborah Burand

As the first four chapters of this book have shown, housing finance is a critical tool for making adequate housing available and affordable. Yet the amount of capital necessary to finance the growing need for affordable housing is nowhere near to being met. Attracting more investments into housing microfinance, and affordable housing finance more generally, requires a strategy that stands on three legs. First, the financial returns and risks need to be more accurately and effectively articulated and shared with investors. Second, the positive social and environmental impacts from

http://dx.doi.org/10.3362/9781780447681.006

adequate, affordable housing need to be rigorously measured, analysed, and publicized. And third, risk mitigants and credit enhancements need to be tapped to ensure that capital flowing into housing microfinance carries financial terms that are commensurate with the perceived risks. These three legs need solid ground to stand on, and investors should be aware that the sector remains nascent in many countries. Where that is the case, building up the relevant practices and market-level infrastructure requires developmental and philanthropic funds above and beyond investment capital.

This chapter advances the three-legged strategy by presenting real examples that illustrate how investors have successfully increased capital to fuel affordable housing finance in emerging markets. They have done this by deploying a variety of funding instruments that range from debt and equity to off-balance sheet financings, such as securitizations. The examples presented also shed light on the varying roles played by public sector funders: multilateral funders like the International Finance Corporation (IFC), bilateral development funders like Agence Française de Développement (AFD), and local government funders like the National Housing Bank (NHB) of India.

Funding challenges

Raising capital for housing finance loans can be challenging. At the risk of over-simplifying, it has to do with the inherent problems of moving international capital into and out of emerging markets. Think of this as a 'neighbourhood' business problem. If the neighbourhood is in bad shape (dangerous road conditions, poorly policed, and ill-lit), customers won't visit. Or, at least, they won't without some well-intentioned companions accompanying them – in this case credit enhancements or other risk mitigants. But once the investment is made, the neighbourhood becomes more attractive.

Understanding investor needs can also be challenging. In a 2018 report, investors made it clear that by funding financial inclusion they are seeking both a financial return on their investments and evidence that their investments are generating a positive social return (CSFI, 2018). But these same investors take different views about which risks (financial or social) are most troubling: 'Some respondents concentrated on risks that could jeopardise profits, such as bad debts, rising costs and excessive competition. Others focused on risks that might deflect their investments from the goal of financial inclusion, such as political interference, poor regulation and mission drift' (CSFI, 2018: 12). This chapter illuminates some of these challenges faced by investors, including segmenting housing loans in a microfinance portfolio, differentiating between housing microfinance and micro-mortgage loans, tracking loan use, and defining home improvement and its social impact.

Another set of challenges arise specific to funding new financial products in microfinance institutions (MFIs) or base-of-the-pyramid financial institutions.

Even investors who have got comfortable with the risk/return proposition of investing in microfinance institutions may balk at funding the launch of products with a limited track record, such as housing microfinance. Some may not understand the risk/return profile of these new housing-focused products and make the mistake of thinking that they will not perform as well as more conventional forms of microfinance, like working capital loans. This is where investors are especially well positioned to combine their investments with sector know-how and technical assistance grants that can provide the specialized experience of individuals and organizations that have implemented housing microfinance in many different markets. The MicroBuild case in this chapter provides an excellent example of this approach.

The specific features and terms of housing microfinance products (as previously discussed in Chapter 4) can also mean that the sources of capital that fund microfinance for working capital may not work well for housing microfinance loans. This discrepancy can take shape in currency mismatches, term/maturity mismatches, and even cost-of-capital challenges such that housing microfinance loans are not affordable for their intended beneficiaries. There are, of course, workarounds that institutions can use to adapt funding to purposes different from those originally intended by their investors (like automatically renewing loans to make the term seem shorter than it is), but these workarounds are inefficient, often expensive, and, worse still, can increase other risks such as liquidity and currency.

Taken together, these challenges represent a series of missed opportunities to raise capital to fund new housing loan products for poor customers living in emerging markets. No wonder the financing of housing has been slow in ramping up!

New approaches to attract investors

Fortunately, a range of approaches and financial instruments, like those presented in this chapter, can ensure a good fit for a variety of investor needs. These include debt and equity investments, geographical exposure, and currency risk appetite. There are also a variety of ways to mitigate risks so as to catalyse capital flows (with appropriate terms) into housing finance. But scaling is not a problem that can be resolved simply by contract or financial engineering. Only by demonstrating the impact returns that are achievable with housing finance products will the sector attract a diverse group of public and private investors who, together, can bring an appropriate blend of capital to the table. In many countries this requires investing in market and institutional capacity, which is a theme that flows across nearly all the examples in this chapter: a local public entity like the NHB sets the rules and priorities that shape the sector; multi- and bilateral Development Finance Institutions (DFIs) support both public and private institutions not only by providing capital for on-lending, but building capacity in the sector; and private funds that combine finance with built-in technical assistance enable financial institutions to improve and expand their affordable housing products. In every case, the investor brings to the table not only capital, but their unique expertise and deep focus on expanding housing access to the poor.

The good news on this front is that housing finance is attracting a growing number of impact investors: investors seeking to generate both financial and social returns. According to the Global Impact Investment Network's (GIIN) survey of impact investors, 39 per cent of those surveyed had invested in housing, with 7 per cent of their impact assets under management devoted to housing (GIIN, 2019). Many of these investors are seeking more than financial returns. In a different survey, all of the impact investors observed that 'social impact' was a key motivation for their investments in affordable housing (Habitat for Humanity, 2017). Other notable motivations such as diversification of portfolios and financial returns, were less unanimous.

The clear impact focus of those investors is encouraging because affordable housing finance can deliver social impact. And it suggests that there is another important piece to attracting more investments into this sector: robust social impact evaluations of housing investments. The GIIN study uncovered some levels of dissatisfaction by current investors with the impact stories being told about housing. Of the surveyed investors, 21 per cent noted a need for 'better targeting of certain groups and geographies', and 17 per cent wanted 'better reporting on social impact'. So how are investors currently measuring the impacts of housing? Most use standard evaluation frameworks, drawing on performance metrics found in GIIN's IRIS framework for reporting social impact, which is very *output*-oriented, as opposed to *outcome*-oriented. Common impact metrics include performance indicators such as the number of housing loans disbursed and number of beneficiaries reached. Some investors, however, are starting to look at the social impacts that arise from improved access to affordable housing. These include environmental impacts like water and energy consumption, and waste production. Still others are looking at how improved housing can contribute to the quality of life for the broader community, and to progress on the Sustainable Development Goals (SDGs).

As stated above, the strategy for attracting more investments into housing microfinance should stand on three legs: knowledge sharing about the financial returns and risks of investing in affordable housing finance; rigorous measurement and analysis of positive social and environmental impacts that it can generate; and strategic use of risk mitigants and credit enhancements to ensure appropriate financial terms (such as pricing, currency, and tenor). In many markets the three legs of the strategy will be most effective when combined with non-financial support aimed at building the market to support a pipeline of investments and developing institutional capacity to deliver affordable housing finance, and beyond. Implementing such a strategy will not be easy, but the prize – a larger pool of appropriate capital flowing into housing microfinance – is well worth it, as the examples that follow demonstrate.

The microbuild fund: Private debt in housing microfinance

Claudia Rojas, Triple Jump

In 2011 only a few of Triple Jump's 166 investees (mostly microfinance institutions in emerging markets) offered specialized housing loans, despite the estimation that as much as 20 per cent of microfinance business lending was *de facto* used for housing purposes. To address this demand, Triple Jump and Habitat for Humanity International (HFHI) jointly launched the MicroBuild Fund in 2012. The fund was created to fill a critical gap in financial inclusion: the gap between the need for loans that could improve clients' housing conditions and the microfinance institutions that were not addressing this need. It was initially intended to be a source of long-term social investment capital for some 30 to 40 financial institutions to expand their housing microfinance portfolios, demonstrating and showcasing to the wider microfinance sector the viability and scale opportunities provided by housing microfinance.

A key feature of the fund is a complementary technical assistance (TA) programme to help financial intermediaries develop and improve their housing products to better meet end-clients' needs. Funded by HFHI, the TA programme is delivered by its advisory arm, the Terwilliger Center for Innovation in Shelter (TCIS). Its team, with over two decades of experience developing and implementing housing microfinance programmes around the world, verifies the institution's commitment towards making housing an organizational priority, helps with a tailor-made approach designed to tackle the organization's specific needs, and works to ensure that institutions provide housing support services to borrowers (see Chapter 4 for a fuller discussion of housing support services).

The MicroBuild Fund has a distinctive public–private partnership formula. Not only does it have a government agency, two private social investors, and a foundation as stakeholders, but it also includes the world's largest non-profit building organization. The fund is capitalized by USD 10 million of equity and USD 90 million of debt from the Overseas Private Investment Corporation (OPIC), the development finance institution of the US government.[1] As a sponsor of the MicroBuild Fund, HFHI owns a majority equity stake of 51 per cent and, through the support of its high-net-worth donors, provides a 10 per cent first loss guarantee. Other investors include: Omidyar Network, a US-based private social investor; MetLife Foundation; and Triple Jump, which is also MicroBuild's investment advisor. HFHI has committed 10 per cent of total capitalization to provide technical assistance.

The MicroBuild Fund closed its first phase of USD 50 million in August 2012 and the second phase was closed in May 2016, doubling the fund size to USD 100 million. The launch of the MicroBuild Fund with HFHI has been one of Triple Jump's most successful ventures in recent years. From its first disbursements in August 2012, through the beginning of 2020, MicroBuild successfully leveraged the fund's capital 1.3 times, disbursing almost USD 135 million.

This funding enabled 54 financial service providers in 31 countries to supply tailored services to their clients while improving their credit risk and, most importantly, unlocking opportunities for long-term social housing investments for an estimated 173,000 households and 866,000 individuals.

In 2016, the MicroBuild Fund received the OPIC Impact Award, and in 2017 the Classy Award for leading a successful programme that positively impacts access to finance.

Operations

Given the unique construction of the MicroBuild Fund, its operations entail more coordination and initial work to ensure that the financial interme- diary is ready to receive a loan, compared with traditional microfinance debt funds. To accomplish this, the fund's operations (after many iterations) allow for a streamlined coordination between Triple Jump's investment teams and HFHI's area offices, employing monthly calls to identify potential MFIs to be included in the MicroBuild investment pipeline. Prospective MFIs are pre-screened, assessed, and scored based on both financial and housing microfinance related criteria. Very similar to the other mandates and funds administered by Triple Jump, three key financial dimensions were chosen to serve as the minimum criteria for the proposed MFI investments: MFIs need to have achieved or be on track towards achieving operational self-sustain- ability, demonstrate acceptable portfolio quality, and have a reasonable equity base.

Unique to the MicroBuild Fund, four additional dimensions specific to housing microfinance were chosen as minimum criteria for proposed MFI investments: (1) the management and board of the borrowing institution should demonstrate commitment to housing microfinance; (2) the housing product should be clearly identifiable in the management information system of the institution as opposed to only being documented by an *ex-post* evaluation of the use of a credit by the financial institution's clients; (3) the housing portfolio should be at least USD 300,000 at the time of investment or show a track record of at least three months of providing sustainable and scalable housing microfinance products; and (4) there should be a willingness to introduce at least basic housing support services (HSS) to the customer (for example, handing out brochures to clients that provide advice on simple, high-quality construction techniques). HSS can be developed by HFHI as part of its technical assistance.

Once the institution has demonstrated these basic indicators and has passed a standard investment review (compliance, country and institutional risk review, etc.), the process moves to due diligence, which differs significantly from the typical process. Due diligence visits are conducted by two teams: the Triple Jump investment team and the HFHI technical assistance team. These may be conducted simultaneously and often last three days, including at least six housing client visits. After the due diligence visit, each team prepares its report: the HFHI team prepares a technical assistance report, which is reviewed by an internal technical assistance committee. When approved, this TA report is then sent together with Triple Jump's Investment Report to the MicroBuild Investment Committee, which is composed of six members, two from HFHI and four external, experienced members from the impact investing sector, the financial sector, and academia.

Once an investment has been approved by the Investment Committee and disbursed, the investee receives institutional TA and sends monthly financial and social reports, including housing information, which are monitored by both teams during the life of the loan. The monthly calls established between Triple Jump and HFHI area offices also serve to monitor the progress of the technical assistance and are determinants for the approval of possible subsequent loans. This detailed assessment and close monitoring process, with its strong and unyielding focus on the housing-specific aspects of the programme being financed, has assured the best possible portfolio quality and housing impact for MicroBuild.

Portfolio evolution

During its more than seven years of operation, the fund has exceeded its targets, both in terms of the number of financial intermediaries financed and country outreach. Having placed over USD 135 million in loan capital to date, as of December 2019, the fund has a portfolio of USD 81 million outstanding to 38 microfinance institutions across 24 countries.[2]

However, MicroBuild's regional distribution has shifted during this time. The Caucasus and Central Asia was one of the first regions where the fund invested, but its share of the fund decreased from 44 per cent in 2014 to only 11 per cent in 2017 (while Asia and the Pacific region grew by a factor of 18 during the same period). In 2016 and 2017, Azerbaijan investees were hit

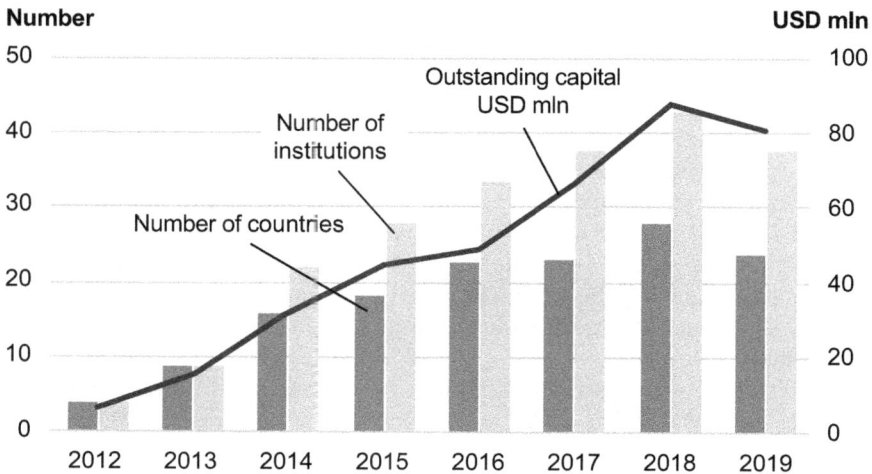

Figure 5.1 MicroBuild fund's growth

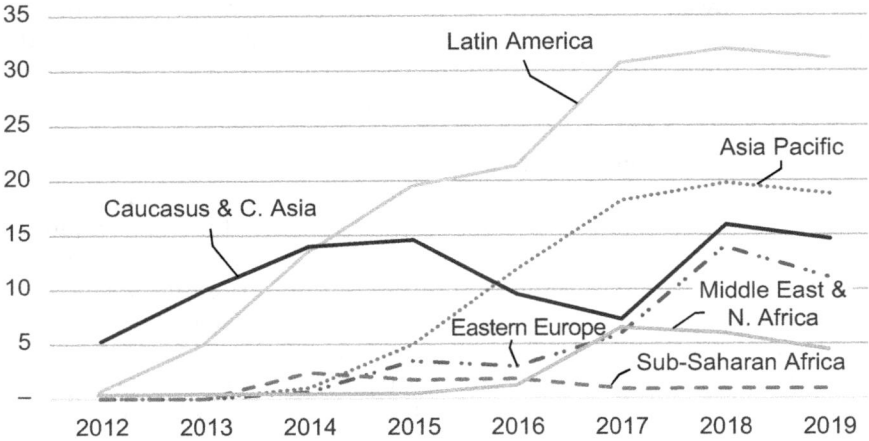

Figure 5.2 MicroBuild capital outstanding, USD million

by two unexpected local currency devaluations and adverse regulation on interest rates, and Tajikistan suffered from the indirect effects of the crisis in Russia, which represented a very important source of remittances.

Over the last two years, Asia Pacific has remained as the best performing market and the largest region for MicroBuild with USD 18.8 million outstanding. MicroBuild has been most successful in Cambodia and India, two of the most established microfinance markets in the region, where MFIs offer a wide range of housing products and there are dedicated housing finance companies, several of which operate in the affordable housing niche. In India, the government has made financial inclusion a top priority, and the credit quality of financial intermediaries has surpassed that of even some of the best performing microfinance markets. Other markets where MicroBuild has been active to finance first movers are Mongolia, Timor Leste, and Sri Lanka, where HFHI's housing expertise has been key in helping MFIs establish new housing microfinance programmes.

In Latin America, MicroBuild loans *with* technical assistance have experienced great success, as together they have allowed MFIs to further professionalize operations and optimize their housing loan products. The fact that MicroBuild offers both USD and local currency loans has played a critical role in the fund's regional success. Currently, Latin America accounts for 38 per cent of the fund's outstanding portfolio, with South America alone having the second largest regional exposure, after Asia Pacific, mainly due to a few large MFIs in Colombia, Ecuador, and Peru demanding large-ticket borrowings.

Eastern Europe is another important area of growth, with three countries – Albania, Bosnia & Herzegovina, and Moldova – being added to MicroBuild's portfolio since 2017. This has contributed to regional growth of 91 per cent, to reach USD 11 million as of December 2019.

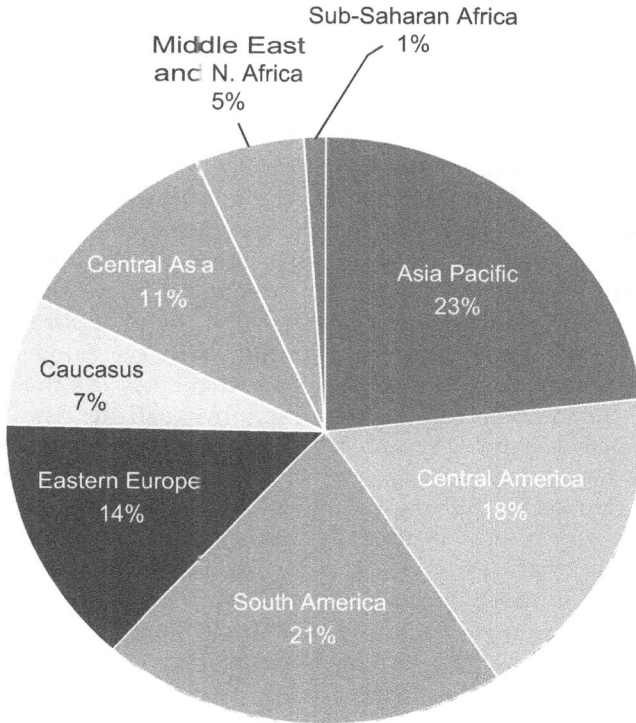

Figure 5.3 MicroBuild fund regional distribution, as of year-end 2019

In contrast, sub-Saharan Africa continues to suffer from macro-economic and political challenges that contribute to volatile currencies and high hedging costs. General institutional weakness (such as poor governance, low staff capacity, and low asset quality), but also less capacity to absorb housing loans, has limited the growth of the MicroBuild Fund on the continent. On the other hand, the Middle East and North Africa (especially Jordan, Lebanon, and Palestine), while an unstable and volatile region, has strong players and market leaders, and an enabling environment for international funding. In this region, MicroBuild has been an early mover, as opposed to other microfinance investment vehicles that are just recently increasing their exposure in the region.

Risk profile

The credit risk profile of the MicroBuild Fund remains stable at BB+, which is similar to, or slightly better than, that of other Triple Jump funds given their different risk nature, regional focus, client segments, and goals. This may be because of the particularly stringent requirements of the fund. Moreover, the introduction of a housing portfolio tends to improve the overall portfolio quality of the investee MFI: housing loan portfolio at risk is 2 per cent lower than that of the overall portfolio.[3] In part, this is a reflection of the overall higher credit quality of housing loans (see Chapter 4 for detail), though it also reflects the value of technical assistance, ensuring housing products are appropriately designed for the operating environment and clientele of each institution.

The difference in financial performance between an MFI's housing loans and the rest of their portfolio is even larger for distressed institutions. For the few institutions in MicroBuild's portfolio currently facing macro-economic and/or political problems (for example, in the West Bank and Nicaragua), housing loans perform six times better, with portfolio at risk of 5.25 per cent for housing loans compared to 31 per cent for the total portfolio. This is strong evidence that housing loans perform well even under distressed situations as clients tend to value the place where they live more than any other asset. In addition to providing or improving shelter, HMF has other benefits such as improving quality of life: sanitation and health, security of tenure, and happiness.

Housing microfinance loans also differ from traditional microfinance in their longer tenors. In order to match the tenors of the housing products offered by the fund's investees, the current MicroBuild portfolio likewise features longer tenors than most: an average of 4.2 years compared with 3.1 years from other funds administered by Triple Jump.

However, longer maturity also increases currency risk when investing in local currency. This risk is managed using three strategies: 48 per cent of MicroBuild's portfolio is invested in US dollars; 41 per cent is hedged commercially; 10.7 per cent is exposed to six local currencies, out of which 5 per cent is leveraged by a dedicated facility designed specifically for MicroBuild and funded by the Hilti Foundation, which has partnered with HFHI since 2012. The facility pays the hedging costs for loans disbursed to MFIs in markets where high hedging costs and local currency pricing would otherwise make the fund's offering uncompetitive. The facility was developed under the premise that a portfolio of many different currencies can successfully diversify away the risk and volatility of a foreign exchange position. By enabling investments in new countries and new currencies, the facility has driven a large part of the fund's growth and will remain an important feature of MicroBuild's investment strategy.

Outlook

Scheduled to mature in 2026, the MicroBuild Fund is approaching its final phase. Triple Jump expects to continue building on the successful symbiosis of lending bundled with technical assistance, bringing the fund as close to fully invested as possible and maintaining a high exposure mainly in Latin America and Asia and the Pacific, anticipating solid portfolio growth and high social return ahead.

Triple Jump and HFHI are also looking for other investment options to continue supporting housing microfinance while contributing to a vibrant market that moves MFIs' current investment in housing from an approximate 2 to 10 per cent of their portfolios, thus providing an additional USD 3.6 billion of housing finance, and reaching an estimated 7.2 million people. Based on Triple Jump's experience with the MicroBuild Fund, future initiatives should focus on further adaptation to regional reality and needs, such as lending in local currencies, longer tenors, larger loan amounts, higher risk investments, even more patient capital, and mechanisms to enable institutional borrowing at more affordable rates.

NHB: A national apex funder crowding in private investment

R.V. Verma, National Housing Bank, India

Despite many programmes from multiple governments, 18.6 million households lack access to housing in India, most of them poor families working in the informal sector. Recognizing that a different path was needed in both construction and financing, the government began a multi-year effort to begin to narrow this deficit, and the National Housing Bank (NHB) is a key part of this effort (other aspects of the policy reform are described in the India Deep Dive section of Chapter 2).

The policies, programmes, and strategies of the NHB have evolved since its founding in 1987, but are always guided by the core principles of its Charter:

- To recognize that a vast majority of the people in the lower-income segment of the population are critically dependent on loans/credit at affordable terms for their housing needs.
- To develop the institutional mechanisms and build capacity for microfinance in the housing sector to serve this market segment.
- To design supportive policies and products for effective role of microfinance in delivering housing solutions
- To explore and promote market-based sustainable housing solution for people with small means and the vast growing number in the informal sector.
- To develop a sound, deep, vibrant, and inclusive housing finance system and mortgage industry to meet the needs of the unserved and the underserved.
- To develop the mortgage industry by creating the right market infrastructure and catalysing and creating opportunities for borrowers, lenders, builders, and investors in the sector.

Until the second decade of the 21st century, housing finance in India was limited to mortgages issued to middle- and upper-income households with formal employment. These households presented excellent growth and profits for the country's mortgage lenders: regulated banks and specialized housing finance companies (HFCs) supervised by the NHB.[4] However, this growth neglected a far larger population segment – the millions of households with small and moderate incomes working in the informal sector, often composed of first-generation migrants to the country's rapidly expanding cities. Without access to affordable housing finance, millions of households were being left behind, with the growing housing deficit as the symptom of an escalating market failure.

Few housing lenders had the requisite skills for accomodating informal incomes, low equity contribution by the borrowers, and other pre-requisites such as formalizing the land collateral and guarantee, validating land title and related documentation, enforcing collateral in the event of foreclosure, and ensuring affordability of loan payments. More challenging still was the absence of a supportive and enabling policy and regulatory framework for the finance and construction industries to cater to this segment of the population.

Fostering a housing finance revolution

Drawing on its experience working with the HFCs, the NHB sought to bring the private market into this sector, building a network of specialized institutions and promoting the industry's capacity to deal with the housing needs of all sections of the population, with focus on the economically weaker and disadvantaged section of the society. The NHB nurtured and encouraged housing finance including through partnerships with commercial banks and microfinance institutions, but it was a new breed of affordable housing finance companies (A-HFCs), created by promoters with the explicit goal of serving the households being left behind, that represented an innovation where India emerged as the global leader.

These A-HFCs were experimenting with the micro-mortgage product. By extending financial support right from their start-up stage, together with capacity building and market infrastructure initiatives, the NHB created the

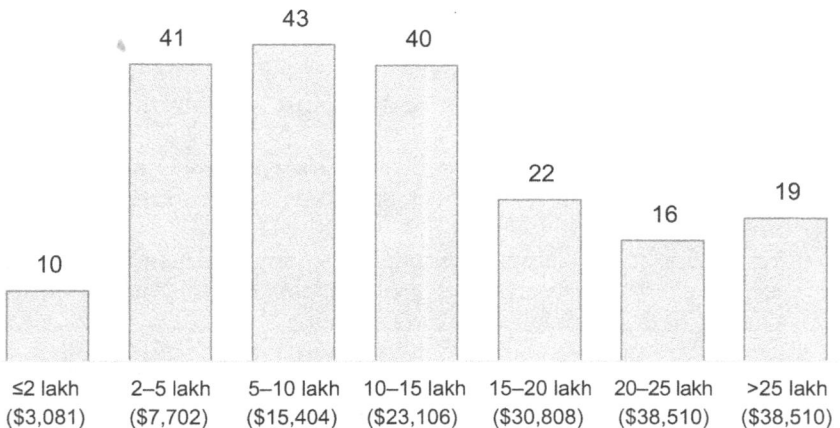

Figure 5.4 Number of individual housing loans funded by NHB refinance disbursements 2017–2018 (000s)
Source: NHB Annual Report 2017–18; Exchange rate from Oanda.com as of 31 Mar 2018

space in which this new sector could develop. NHB funding to HFCs was targeted to those with the following social impact objectives: at least 50 per cent of the housing loan portfolio composed of loans below Rs. 0.5 million (USD 7,000), and a lending policy with a clear focus on affordable housing for the informal sector and low income borrowers, including women and rural households (some of these could be carried out under the government's subsidy-linked programme).

The focus on lower-income households is apparent from NHB's refinancing portfolio, as shown in Fig 5.4, which demonstrates a strong emphasis on lower-income and lower-middle class families. Seventy per cent of its loans are under USD 23,106. The ratio of loan size to annual household income for housing loans is about four to one. Considering that such loans are usually made to households with multiple income earners, this suggests that the upper bound of the bulk of the NHB's clientele is slightly above the average in India, that is to say, a household income of just below USD 6,000.[5]

Financing schemes of NHB

NHB operates a number of wholesale financing schemes to support on-lending to individuals, with incentives aimed towards lending to low-income borrowers. Institutions covered under NHB funding include commercial banks, housing finance companies, regional rural banks, cooperative banks, and microfinance institutions. Due to their leading role in the country's housing finance sector, the primary recipients of NHB's financing are the country's banks and HFCs:

Table 5.1 Cumulative NHB refinance disbursement as at 30 June 2018

Institution type	Percentage share
Scheduled commercial banks	51
Housing finance companies	46
Others	3

Source: NHB Annual Report 2017–2018

Funding from the NHB carries a concessional rate of interest and meets the tenor requirements that enable on-lending institutions to mitigate their asset-liability mismatch risk. The portfolio of the NHB's funding products and schemes is too long to detail here, but the below list is largely representative of its activities:

- **Affordable Housing Fund**: Created with a corpus of Rs. 100 billion (USD 1.4 billion) to help HFCs and banks leverage their resources and capacity to lend to low income households.
- **Special refinance for urban low-income housing**. Provides housing loans of up to Rs. 500,000 (USD 7,000) to urban households

with (mainly informal) annual incomes below Rs. 200,000 (USD 2,800). The loans improve affordability by providing refinancing at fixed interest rate for a term of 10–15 years, ensuring lower monthly payments while also protecting both lenders and borrowers against interest rate volatility. The loans can be used for a broad set of housing-related uses, from purchase and new unit construction to renovation and up-gradation of existing dwellings. Funded by the World Bank under a special credit line of USD 100 million, the NHB lends these funds either directly or through intermediaries. A line of credit supports the informal sector through micro-mortgages. A total sum of Rs. 5,881 million (USD 82.5 million) has been disbursed across 17 HFCs. With the successful implementation of the scheme, a second line of credit from the World Bank to the NHB is being explored. (Note: since March/April 2019, the special refinance for urban low-income housing was merged into the Affordable Housing Fund.)

- **Prime Minister's Housing Programme (PMAY)**: Concessional funding with a subsidized end-client interest rate of 6.5 per cent, targeting individuals belonging to the economically weaker section (EWS: defined as having annual household income below Rs. 300,000 (USD 4,200)) and low income group (LIG: income between Rs. 300,000 and 600,000; USD 4,200–8,400). Can be used for housing loans for new construction as well as incremental improvement of existing dwellings.

- **Credit Risk Guarantee Fund Trust for Low-Income Housing**: This default guarantee scheme is aimed at mitigating credit risk and encouraging HFCs and banks to expand their housing lending to informal and low-income borrowers. Eligible loans must be below Rs. 800,000 (USD 11,219), with guarantee covering up to Rs. 500,000 (USD 7,000) for borrowers without any collateral security. Smaller loans of Rs. 200,000–500,000 (USD 2,800–7,000) are covered at the higher rate of maximum 80 per cent, while loans below Rs. 200,000 are covered up to 90 per cent. Eligible loans may include both purchased property as well as home improvement and expansion.

Leveraging NHB funding to scale up housing finance

The NHB has been able to exert significant influence on the housing finance sector to serve households that have long been excluded from the formal mortgage market. Simultaneously, the NHB's signal of affirmation and approval of the lenders, especially the housing finance companies, have served to catalyse both equity and debt investment for these HFCs from multiple channels. One example of such an outside investor is the Caspian fund described later in this chapter.

With multiple channels of support, including fiscal, regulatory, and NHB refinancing, housing finance in India has seen very positive growth. Combined housing loan disbursements from banks and HFCs averaged 19 per cent annual growth between FY 2011 and FY 2018. Growth among HFCs has

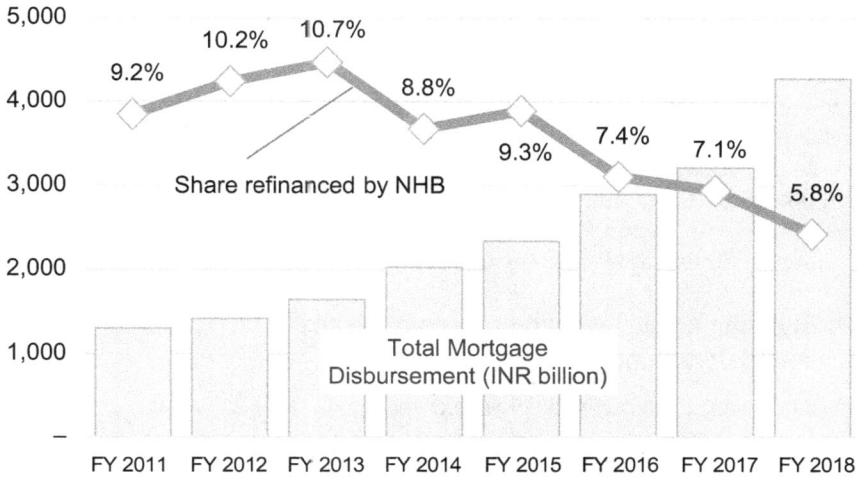

Figure 5.5 Mortgage disbursements by HFCs and public sector banks in India

been greater still, with disbursements averaging 24 per cent annual growth during the period. More recently, there has been a large crowding into the HFC sector, with the number of HFCs growing from 62 in March 2015 to 95 in December 2018.

Throughout this period, the NHB has seen its role greatly leveraged. Even as its refinancing disbursements grew by an average of 11 per cent annually, its share of total disbursements has in fact declined, from 9–10 per cent during the years 2011–2015 to just 5.8 per cent by 2018. Its role in the market remains instrumental, particularly with respect to lending to poor and underserved households, but the NHB has succeeded in crowding in lending from the private sector, which is now the source of the vast majority of funding for housing loans.

One of the elements that has enabled NHB to leverage its role in the provide sector is its unique position as a statutory body wholly owned by the central bank, giving it the lowest risk rating and thus able to raise low-cost funds in the market. Other sources of the NHB's funds include the government's budgetary allocation (Affordable Housing Fund) and government-allocated bonds with tax benefits for investors, and borrowing from banks and international finance institutions and development banks, including the World Bank, KfW, DFID, and AFD (see the section on AFD later in this chapter for details).

Conclusion

The NHB has succeeded in bringing its multiple strengths towards the urgent need of providing housing finance to low- and informal-income households in India. It holds a strong position in both international and local capital markets, including as the preferred local partner for development finance institutions seeking to support housing in India. Its role as standard-setter and regulator of HFCs, and as the institution responsible for implementing and delivering a number of government housing finance programmes and subsidies, has enabled it to crowd-in private sector actors and greatly leverage its direct impact.

Despite the strengths of the NHB and the housing finance system it has incubated, solving the massive housing needs in a country the size of India will take more effort still. The NHB's funding of housing microfinance offered by MFIs for the type of self-building that Nikhil and Panna undertook in Chapter 3, for example, remains minimal.

IFC: Building a housing market, the experience of a multilateral funder

W. Britt Gwinner, International Finance Corporation

As a member of the World Bank Group, International Finance Corporation (IFC) seeks to contribute to the Bank's two goals of ending extreme poverty and promoting shared prosperity, by creating markets that address the biggest development challenges of our time. Housing is one of those challenges, and IFC works to support the entire value chain for housing in developing countries: from land markets to building materials, residential construction, and housing finance. For more than 30 years, IFC has supported the expansion of residential mortgage lending in more than 45 countries, ranging from Argentina to Indonesia and Uganda.

To catalyse the development of sound and widely accessible housing finance markets, IFC:

- Invests in financial institutions and mobilizes capital across the globe, serving as a source of long-term funding;
- Provides advice to financial institutions to strengthen their capacity in housing finance;
- Works with regulatory agencies to improve the enabling environment; and
- Promotes housing as an important asset class, encouraging investors back into the sector following a financial crisis.

Creating markets in under-developed segments where there is a lot of need, like housing, requires significant upstream work and staff time compared with more developed sectors. A typical residential development transaction starts by finding a sponsor with sufficient risk appetite who wants to build housing units affordable to moderate- and low-income families. The land must be located where acquiring and transferring title, building structures, filing liens, and all the other processes required to develop housing, are functional. A bank will then need to be found that is ready to finance and sell the units. Knitting together these types of deals has always been part of the role of IFC, but in recent years an increased focus on market creation as a strategy has led to a greater willingness to invest the time required to do the upstream work on laws and regulations. IFC also spends more on technical assistance where markets are under-developed, particularly in the harder to reach and more fragile countries of sub-Saharan Africa, the Maghreb, and Western Asia, among others.[6]

Financing options

As a multilateral development finance institution, IFC has a lot of flexibility in the type of finance it can provide, and it can adapt its role depending on market need and stage of development. Depending upon circumstances, IFC may invest in equity, debt, or hybrid instruments, and IFC has pioneered capital market instruments for housing in a number of countries. When making an equity investment, IFC expects an equity return; when providing debt, a return of capital plus interest at market rates.

Equity

In terms of equity, IFC has financed greenfield non-bank housing lenders to encourage investment where there is demand but a lack of market participants. India has been a major market for IFC. Eight years ago there were several HFCs entering the Indian market but they were not lending to informally employed individuals or households, where the demand is greatest.[7] Instead, they were trying to copy the success of mortgage lenders HDFC Bank and Dewan Housing Finance Ltd (DHFL), which successfully and importantly focus on formal sector lending.[8]

These large, formal housing lenders with diverse portfolios can help illustrate the role of the IFC in market development. The typical HDFC target client may be a recent engineering graduate working for a large company, with a good salary, who wants to buy a relatively large flat in a nice development in Pune or downtown Mumbai. In contrast, DHFL's target client would also be formally employed, but with a slightly lower salary, and would be looking for an apartment in the lower-cost suburbs of either city.

In the 2000s, new HFCs were looking to copy these successful models and were similarly leery of lending to the informal sector. To encourage the market, a joint venture between IFC and DHFL created Aadhar Housing Finance Limited, which began its operations in lower-income states of India, financing those who are steadily but *informally* employed – carpenters, taxi drivers, plumbers, carpenters, masons. Their incomes may be sufficient to afford housing, but without the documentation that formal employment provides. Aadhar's success in this market has led to many imitators.

Because the focus is on developing the market and bringing other sponsors and investors to the table IFC is never the sole investor. Its investment is limited to 20–25 per cent of total project costs, always a minority. IFC's exit is built into the initial agreement, usually implemented through a trade sale or initial public offering (IPO), with the expectation that new investors will buy out IFC once its role is complete. The timeline is flexible, usually a window of 7–10 years, but without the *requirement* and hence the time pressure to leave that is typical of closed-end private equity firms. IFC needs to recycle its capital, but the exit decision is based on an assessment of whether IFC has completed its role at time of exit.

Debt

IFC provides senior and subordinated debt to lenders, and it supports capital markets instruments such as covered bonds and securitization. Lenders must be established, with capacity to repay the debt, and the funds must be used for housing market development. IFC has provided senior secured and unsecured credit lines for mortgage lending in countries such as Kenya, Turkey, India, Russia, Vietnam, and Panama. In Colombia, IFC played a key role in developing a robust local currency market for the securitization of mortgage debt through its client Titularizadora Colombiana. IFC supported cross-border mortgage-covered bonds for Turkish banks looking to diversify funding sources.

Process

Investment in a sector like housing begins when the World Bank group conducts a country-level diagnostic of the overall macro-economic environment and organization of the private sector (country private sector diagnostics, or CPSD). The CPSD helps identify what the World Bank Group could do to strengthen the value chain, and what firms are active: banks, non-bank finance companies, developers, builders, and others. Then a micro-level analysis is made of the private sector to determine what firms are available to finance.

For example, in Côte d'Ivoire property developers are willing to work with the low-income market segment if home-purchase finance is in place, but they are too small for IFC to finance directly. In such a case, IFC can finance banks that, in turn, finance developers. Once the developer has grown sufficiently, IFC can lend directly to them. IFC's relationship with the same bank can facilitate finance of mortgages, which encourages the developer to build more. This ability to develop the market on both the supply and demand side – working with banks to provide financing to both developers and home buyers – gives IFC a significant advantage in pursuing its market development mission.

Risk

Retail housing finance requires an additional risk assessment, beyond the standard for equity (capacity of the market to support the equity investment and the return expectation) and debt (corporate governance, credit risk, CAMEL indicators, promoter experience, and financial depth). Retail mortgage lending is a volume- and system-driven business, and business processes and systems need to be robust. A retail housing finance investment involves reviewing a random sample of loan files, looking at the record keeping, talking to loan officers, seeing if business processes are tight and are followed in practice, and looking at systems that back up those processes.

The systems intensity of housing lending is one of the reasons that fintech holds such promise for the sector. To the degree that technology can reduce the labour intensity of housing finance, it will make the industry more efficient, which reduces risk. Mortgage lenders have been intensive users of automation since it became widely available in the 1980s. Large-volume lenders long ago digitized the documents that establish mortgage liens and property ownership. Similarly, automating the credit decision process with reliable data on capacity and willingness to pay is critical to mortgage lenders. Lenders that effectively automate from origination to collection operate with wider profit margins and are better able to detect and respond to payment problems when they come up.

Advisory services

IFC's advisory practice can help potential and existing clients understand their customer base, potential demand, the market context, and to design successful products for their market. In housing, the biggest advisory need is typically in developing the business processes needed to extend and manage long maturity retail credits: up to 20 years for mortgage lenders, and 5–10 years for MFIs. IFC's advisory services can help a lender to develop the efficient, automated systems, and robust processes necessary for loan origination and collection.

Another area where advisory services are used is improving corporate governance. IFC asks its financial sector clients to adhere to the Equator Principles of corporate governance.[9] These principles have greatly increased the attention and focus on social/community standards and responsibility, including robust standards for indigenous peoples, labour standards, and consultation with locally affected communities.

Local partners

Generally, the sponsors of an investment where IFC participates are a group of people who want to build locally. IFC looks for sponsors that see the development value as well as the financial payoff. Returns are important because it takes a lot of work and expense on their part, and it can be a struggle to find the necessary resources. An IFC package is intended to help the sponsors succeed, in a way that works for low-income families in the country.

For housing construction, IFC invests in property developers that have a track record of financial success and that show a potential for nationwide growth. One IFC partner is PT Ciputra Residence, one of the largest property builders in Indonesia. For international companies like these, low-cost housing fits in their overall business plan for the country, and IFC can help finance that growth.

However, sponsors of affordable housing finance are extremely limited. Sometimes a broader institutional approach is needed. In Kenya, for example, low cost housing is mostly financed through Savings and Credit Cooperatives (SACCOs), but due to their ownership structure IFC cannot finance them directly. To address this, the World Bank is looking to create a liquidity facility in Kenya (similar to those existing in neighbouring countries), in which IFC can invest, and which will lend to SACCOs. Until then, IFC is focused on advisory services – training SACCOs to help structure the demand for a housing loan product that can work there.

Where formal institutions exist, IFC prefers to work with them as sponsors and investees, but formality is often a luxury in developing markets. If they do not exist, less formal institutions may be acceptable. Microfinance institutions (MFIs), for example, often don't have full banking licences and have limited funding sources. They often lack the asset/liability management systems and other technical skills necessary to assess the capacity and willingness of individuals to repay a loan over a longer period of time, and to manage a longer-term loan book. But sometimes non-bank lenders see a market niche the big banks don't see.

Housing microfinance

IFC has supported housing microfinance (HMF) with advisory and investment services for many years, including projects in Egypt, Afghanistan, Haiti, India, and elsewhere. Generally, housing lending appeals to MFIs that have a successful track record and have developed a strong client base, and that have a vision for growth and lending at longer maturities than traditional micro-enterprise credit.

Often, investment comes after a period of providing advisory services. In India, microlenders like Aavas are making USD 14,000 loans to informally employed people earning just USD 3,000 to USD 4,000 per year, to build or buy completed houses. This is a step away from incremental construction, providing the borrower with a completed home that is hooked up to power, water, and sanitation. Those same lenders are also lending for incremental improvement and construction for individuals who own a parcel of land. IFC is particularly keen on developing the market for fully built houses because it is more efficient and cost effective for an individual to buy a house than it is to build something over 20 years, paying retail prices for building materials and labour.

Challenges

Macro-economic environment

One of the main challenges for long maturity mortgage lending in emerging markets is macro-economic volatility. In a lot of sub-Saharan African countries today, and historically in much of Latin America, high inflation leads to high nominal interest rates and acts a major constraint to long-term finance. In Nigeria and Ghana, long-term financing is currently infeasible because of high inflation. Individuals are not able to afford monthly payments when mortgage rates exceed 16 or 17 per cent.

Institutional issues

Shortcomings in public administrative systems and institutions often act as a barrier to housing finance. A functional retail mortgage market requires reasonably low transactions costs. This implies fees for titling and registration for a piece of real property should not exceed 3.5 to 5 per cent of the value of the property. Titles also need to be generally free from trivial legal challenges; it should be possible to transfer ownership of a piece of property in less than a few days.

Supply

Supply is a huge challenge with much regional variation. In Latin America and some emerging East Asian countries like Vietnam and Philippines there are large, well-capitalized builders who see value in moving closer to the base of the income pyramid and are building housing affordable to that demographic. However, in many places, particularly sub-Saharan Africa, there is almost no construction of units affordable to most households. There, the construction industry is under-capitalized, atomized, and disorganized.

In many countries, lenders that wish to serve lower-income households are stymied because there is very little housing built at a price that the bulk of the population can afford. IFC is trying to promote supply by creating markets – working with local authorities on institutional issues, and promoting South–South solutions, such as bringing larger builders to countries that lack them.

Informality

For IFC to fulfil its goal of creating a housing sector – construction and lending – that serves the bulk of the population, informality needs to be addressed and methods developed that enable lenders to serve the median and lower segments of the population. Otherwise, mass housing is not possible. Seventy per cent of Indonesians are informally employed, and close to 90 per cent in Côte d'Ivoire. Yet the formal housing sector is oriented towards the top 1 to 2 per cent. Kenya is a typical example where the formal sector produces only about 50,000 units each year, at an average price of USD 250,000. This type of housing is not affordable to anyone except the top 1 per cent. However, large banks don't have the experience needed to evaluate the loan payment capacity of informally employed individuals, and typically are not interested in the costly retooling of their business model and operations to do so.

Successes

Ten years ago, the World Bank and IFC financed several studies on the construction and finance value chain in India. These detailed studies made a business case that housing finance could be a profitable business. At that time, the government of India was also ready to address this issue; there had been a steady push by previous national governments, and several states, to develop new policies for construction, including related issues like titling and registries (see the section on the NHB in this chapter for more on India's policy and regulatory approach). Finding developers and builders interested in the affordable housing segment was challenging, but eventually IFC made some initial investments. Interested lenders were more plentiful: three of the 14 lenders IFC is funding in India are focused on housing microfinance or micro-mortgages: Aavas, Aadhar, and Micro Housing Finance Company.

The early work of creating the market (demonstrating the business case to industry) was important. It required a lot of leg work to find sponsors who desired market growth, understood the business case, and would invest, such as DHFL. But despite their ambition for growth, it took years of relationship building before they were ready to sponsor a deal. A common constraint is the identification of the right people in the organization who are willing to take a risk and lead a new initiative. It took a lot of time, but after financing Aadhar, three or four other companies moved into the market and affordable housing finance is now a dynamic sector.

Box 5.1 Aadhar[10]

Aadhar offers housing finance loans to households earning USD 1,200 to USD 4,800 per year that may not have proof of income, such as self-employed business owners. It offers smaller loans for repairs or incremental construction as well as mortgage loans. Aadhar serves this segment, which is broadly considered excessively risky, with a non-performing loan rate of 0.93 per cent.

Aadhar entered the housing finance market in 2010 as a joint venture between DHFL and IFC. The initial intent was to serve households in lower-income states. In addition to financial support, IFC provided advisory services covering market entry strategy, product design, sales and market approach as well as advice on the risk management framework. In June 2019, DHFL and IFC sold Aadhar in its entirety to the Blackstone Group, Inc.

Aadhar operates in a single industry segment: housing finance. By 30 September 2019, Aadhar had grown to 150,000 clients, its assets under management totalled USD 1.45 billion, and it reached 20 Indian states and union territories.

Loan sizes average USD 11,000, and the tenor ranges from 24 months to 60 months. Eighty per cent of Aadhar's customers have a monthly salary below USD 550.

Microfinance interest rates in India range from 22 to 24 per cent and MFIs require collateral for loans exceeding USD 1,500. For many microfinance clients, the home is also the place of production for their micro or small business. Clients who can improve their housing conditions experience an increased quality of life and well-being and, as a result, become more productive, creative, and satisfied. Those clients who take out HMF loans are considered lower credit risks and more satisfied customers. HMF also allows microfinance institutions to retain existing clients or attract new clients. By offering HMF products, a microfinance institution improves its risk-management framework (especially through diversification and better identification of risks). Because of rising demand for housing finance in South Asia, entering this market offers an unrivalled opportunity for microfinance institutions. They are likely to benefit from enhanced profitability and sustainability of their overall operations.

AFD: A bilateral funder greening housing finance

Lucie Astier Such, Agence Française de Développement, with Daniel Rozas

Agence Française de Développement (AFD) is an inclusive, public financial institution tasked with implementing France's development policy. It makes commitments to projects that genuinely improve the everyday lives of people, in developing and emerging countries and in the French overseas territories. The AFD Group (which includes its investment arm Proparco), works in many sectors (energy, health, housing, biodiversity, water, digital technologies, training), and supports the transition to a safer, more equitable, and more sustainable world. This includes a significant focus on affordable housing, including improving access to housing finance.

As a development institution, AFD's focus is on building or supporting the infrastructure necessary for a healthy housing finance market, in a manner that meets the objectives of sustainable and inclusive development. The AFD Group has developed a strategic framework for financial systems around three principles: access, transition, and consolidation.

Box 5.2 Access, transition, and consolidation

The AFD Group provides financing and technical assistance to financial service providers (FSPs) and others involved in the housing finance value chain to develop and expand financial products that respond to housing finance needs of low-income households, including housing microfinance and micro-mortgages. This can also include providing medium-term financing (bridge loans) to builders and construction companies building housing for low-income residents.

AFD recognizes the critical impact that growing urbanization and cities play in contributing to greenhouse gas (GHG) emissions and climate change. AFD provides financing and technical assistance to a range of actors in the housing finance value chain with the explicit objective of reducing GHG emissions – including through higher energy efficiency building and retrofitting, household-level renewable energy systems, and other housing elements with a strong impact on climate change.

Recognizing the key role that policies and regulations play in facilitating the development of affordable housing finance, AFD is focused on strengthening the architecture of the housing finance system. AFD supports local government entities with the goal of encouraging local markets to provide long-term, local currency funding for affordable housing finance. This is the newest area of focus for AFD.

These three thematic areas provide the framework that guides AFD's support for affordable housing. Often they are interconnected. Enabling access can mean both funding for FSPs and collaboration with government entities, including those that provide wholesale funding for housing. When these involve products that reduce GHG emissions, that involves the transition axis as well.

On the funding side, AFD provides long-term funding (credit lines up to 15 years) to financial institutions and other financial actors. Mostly this is foreign currency funding, but on a case by case basis it can provide local currency to financial institutions. Between 2008 and 2016, AFD disbursed EUR 272 million in loans dedicated to housing finance. Often such loans are accompanied by technical assistance grants to provide training in green building techniques or managing the risks of a housing finance portfolio, to develop new types of products, as well as research and knowledge building that can benefit the housing finance sector more broadly. In total, these grants comprise 5.7 per cent of AFD's lending (EUR 15.5 million).

To better understand how AFD's funding works in practice, the next section considers two examples: National Housing Bank (NHB), India and Fondo Mi Vivienda (FMV), Peru. These are two of AFD's largest investments in housing finance.

National Housing Bank, India

As described earlier in this chapter, NHB plays a unique role in India's housing finance market as both a leading wholesale lender as well as a regulator. In 2015, AFD committed a EUR 100 million non-sovereign credit line along with a EUR 12 million EU-delegated grant facility to NHB to promote affordable green housing. Half of the funds will be directed towards poor and low-income households, as defined by the government of India.

The programme supports NHB in providing more funding to the green housing sector by refinancing developers of eligible green building projects certified by local labels, via banks and HFCs. Such a financial instrument, often referred to as 'bridge' loan, is a key component of low-cost multi-unit housing. Before low-income households can access micro-mortgages and similar financial tools to purchase accommodations, these units must first be built – a process that requires substantial capital. This credit line aims at filling the critical funding gap from when land is acquired until the completed units are sold.

Criteria for these bridge loans include maturities, grace periods, and pricing to ensure uptake and sustainability. In total, 420,000 square metres of new habitable floor are expected to be constructed, benefiting 12,000 households. NHB, and in turn the banks and HFCs it funds, evaluate the economic and technical feasibility of the projects proposed by the developers. Green projects must be certified by GRIHA or IGBC, two Indian labels with established expertise in green housing certification.

The associated technical assistance programme provides targeted skill development for NHB as well as private and public stakeholders (developers, investors, state governments, and homeowners), building their expertise and capacity to implement green housing schemes. The programme also includes efforts to build awareness of the advantages of green construction in order to influence the housing industry, and encourage regulation and public policies that favour green housing and popularize green labelling.

Fondo Mi Vivienda, Peru

Like NHB, the EUR 120 million line of credit to FMV involves a partnership with a government-affiliated entity. FMV is a wholesale Peruvian development bank that provides housing finance through local financial institutions to middle- and low-income households. AFD's line of credit comprises two portions: 60 per cent to fund FMV's traditional credit activities and 40 per cent dedicated to the *Mivivienda Verde* programme – the first green social housing programme in Peru.

Mivivienda Verde was initially conceived as a loan coupled with a voucher designed to compensate for the higher cost of building dwellings that incorporate energy and water efficiency in their construction, thus enabling first-time homeowners to buy certified green social housing. Real estate developers would receive the grant after meeting 13 pre-defined criteria, under the independent supervision of an international certification firm.

However, in response to limited demand and the constraints faced by this nascent market, FMV and the Ministry of Housing added a substantial reduction of interest rates for mortgages funding green certified housing under the programme (2.1 per cent below the standard refinancing rate offered to banks). This rate reduction, combined with extensive private and public communication campaigns, led to a steep increase in disbursements and fostered the emergence of a new market in green housing. A stock of 45,000 houses are to be certified, and the delivery of more than 1,500 certified buildings is also on the way.

Given the current success of the programme among all major stakeholders (banks, real estate developers, and middle-class households) and despite the cost of voucher and interest rate discounts, FMV and the Peruvian government have decided to continue the programme. A second phase of the programme, with a combined EUR 150 million funding from AFD and two other bilateral funders, is currently being implemented, aimed at adding new and more stringent sustainability criteria and improvements to the programme, such as bioclimatic analysis, recycled materials, and adaptation to climatic zones. It will also aim to create a more sustainable financial scheme for FMV, including the mobilization of Peru's housing budget and mainstreaming of green building criteria into other FMV programmes used by banks and real estate developers.

The programme has had substantial impact: Peruvian households seeking affordable housing are shifting their preference towards 'green' affordable housing over traditional construction, which has spurred banks and developers to focus on serving this demand. The scale of the programme and the shift in demand it has created has spurred consolidation in the green construction market and introduction of new construction practices, as well as decreased prices of sustainable building materials.

Conclusion

These two examples that represent the bulk of AFD's funding for housing finance highlight the critical role of government. Neither of these were projects that would have attracted commercial funding, especially not at the outset of the programme. But both are aimed at catalysing markets towards important goals: encouraging markets to serve low-income households that can afford housing but have historically been largely unserved, and transitioning towards building practices that are more environmentally sustainable. Over time, such investments have the potential to change markets so that commercial actors – including investors – similarly shift their focus, making green construction for low-income households a self-perpetuating market practice. And that, after all, is AFD's development mission.

Is securitization right for housing microfinance?

Vinod Kothari

Securitization is the process of transforming financial assets with receivables into marketable securities. In this way a financial entity, such as a mortgage lender, can raise liquidity by offering these marketable securities to investors, rather than raising debt. By packaging a set of similar assets (such as mortgages) in a special purpose vehicle, a financial entity can allow investors to invest in the underlying assets, while insulating them from the bankruptcy or distress risk of the financial entity itself. Ratings of these securities may be substantially higher than those of the financial entity itself in view of the bankruptcy remoteness and the additional credit enhancements that frequently accompany securitization. Due to the enhanced rating of the securities, the financial entity gains the ability to raise liquidity at rates cheaper than traditional sources of funding.

Use of securitization for refinancing mortgage lending is, in some markets, the commonest way of creating liquidity for mortgage lenders. Almost equally common in India is the use of securitization for refinancing microfinance. This section discusses the current state and the prospects of using securitization in the context of housing microfinance and micro-mortgage lending in India. The Indian securitization market has developed in a somewhat unique direction, as discussed below, but it is interesting to consider the possibilities of integrating housing microfinance with capital markets in a developing market.

The state of housing microfinance in India

Microfinance products in India are regulated to ensure they meet poverty targeting objectives. MFIs are required to maintain at least 85 per cent of their assets in 'qualifying' loans, the restrictions of which greatly limit the scope for housing microfinance. This is a clear disincentive for a microfinance company to pursue housing microfinance. Loans offered by affordable housing finance companies (A-HFCs) are typically for ticket sizes anywhere between Rs. 500,000 (USD 7,025) and Rs. 1,000,000 (USD 14,050), with repayment periods of five years or longer, and likewise fail to meet the definition of housing microfinance.

Housing microfinance is thus offered by neither microfinance companies nor by affordable housing finance companies. The closest equivalent to housing microfinance in India may be a micro-mortgage loan, with an amount of up to Rs. 500,000 (USD 7,050), typically to individuals with informal income, and against title documents which may not constitute a formal mortgage. Such micro-mortgage lending is currently an undefined part of affordable housing finance, rather than microfinance. Some of it is being done by a new breed of micro-lending non-bank finance company (NBFC), often using digital apps or other use of technology. By opting not to be classified as MFIs, these fintech entities are not subject to the asset, income, and loan-size thresholds that restrict MFI lending.

While most of these loans are going to the urban sector, there are some NBFCs focused on rural lending. These rural loans are more likely to be applied for home purchase, home repairs, or progressive construction.

The state of securitization in India

While securitization in India started in 1986, its progress over time has been shaped, directed, stifled, and inspired by regulatory developments. Specifically for the microfinance sector, securitization has been driven by priority sector lending (PSL) – a regulatory stipulation for financial inclusion that requires banks to extend nearly 40 per cent of net credit to certain 'priority sectors':

1. Agriculture
2. Micro, small, and medium enterprises
3. Export credit
4. Education
5. Housing
6. Social infrastructure
7. Renewable energy

Several banks, particularly those which are not focused on branch banking or retail lending, fail to achieve these targets through their own lending.

Instead, to meet these targets, they may invest in PSL-eligible portfolios originated by other financial institutions, including via securitizations. For many MFIs, such PSL-motivated investment has been an important source of funding.

Scope for securitization of micro-mortgage lending

For micro-mortgage lenders, securitizing their loans into PSL-eligible vehicles may offer more potential to increase housing micro-lending, for the following reasons:

- Micro-mortgage lending will satisfy the regulatory definition of PSL-qualifying loans.
- Micro-mortgage lending implies a high degree of diversification and, compared to microfinance, is typically backed by a real asset.
- The default rate in home lending is substantially lower as compared to microfinance or most other forms of mortgage lending.
- The typical repayment term in micro-mortgage lending is higher than in microfinance; hence, investors may get securities for longer durations.
- As compared to microfinance, the restrictions on net interest margins are not applicable to micro-mortgage lending.

While data on micro-mortgage securitizations is limited, the following securitization transactions from affordable housing finance lenders may provide guidance for the potential securitization of micro-mortgage lending.

The underlying loans in these transactions are all small and eligible for PSL requirements. It is also notable that the pools of loans are themselves quite small, which suggests that micro-mortgage lenders need not build up

Table 5.2 Selected A-HFC securitizations in India, 2014–19

Originator	Total issue size (in INR millions)	Year of issue	Performance (%)	
			Pool amortization	Aggregate cash collateral (as percentage of pool principal balance)
Shubham Housing Development Finance Company Private Limited	148.8	2014	74.81 (2019)	9.93 (2019)
India Shelter Finance Corporation Limited	120.1	2014	76.73 (2019)	8.60 (2019)
Aptus Value Housing Finance India Limited	50.3	2015	87.17	13.56
Magma Housing Finance Limited	360.26	2019	NA	NA

Source: Rating rationales issued by ICRA; compiled by the author

large portfolios before attempting securitizations. On the risk side, the excess spread (interest generated by the underlying assets in excess of the interest required for payment to the security-holders) is retained in the security as the pool amortizes, thus mitigating risk of loss to investors. In all four transactions above, this excess spread alone was sufficient to absorb all loan losses. However, these securitizations also include cash collateral placed in reserve by the originator, which provides further protection to investors, even though in these cases the cash collateral was never utilized.

Conclusion

Securitization of micro-mortgage lending seems distinctly feasible in the Indian context, and in the age of fintech-based lending, new NBFCs may find lending for housing far safer, more robust, and more gainful than pure personal loans. Moreover, by qualifying as PSL-eligible assets, these pools may have strong demand, leaving very significant spreads on the table for the originator. Finally, with past experience showing that even small transactions sizes can be effectively securitized, this creates opportunities for even relatively young micro-mortgage lenders to tap securitization as a source of funding.

Caspian: A private equity investor moves into housing microfinance

Mona Kachhwaha[11]

Caspian background

Caspian Impact Investment Advisers is one of the first India-based equity investors in financial inclusion and its various sub-sectors, including affordable housing finance. Because its work has largely paralleled the development of impact investing in India, it is fitting to start with a brief history of Caspian itself, including the role of housing finance within its overall work.

Caspian's first fund, the Bellwether Microfinance Fund, was conceived and funded in 2004–2005, when microfinance was an emerging sector in India and equity investment for MFIs was practically non-existent. Most MFIs operated as non-profits at that time. Bellwether's primary objective was to increase the scale of for-profit microfinance and expand it to underserved geographies and market segments. Among Bellwether's seed stage investments were MFIs like Ujjivan, Janalakshmi, Arohan, and Sonata, all of which went on to achieve scale and success both in impact and commercial terms.

Through its second fund, the India Financial Inclusion Fund (IFIF), which was created in 2008–2009, Caspian's investment focus expanded to cover broader financial inclusion, as a consequence of which Equitas, Micro Housing Finance, Aptus Value Housing Finance, and VBHC Value Homes were added to the portfolio. Caspian was either the first or the second investor in each of these companies. IFIF also made follow-on investments in some of

Bellwether's investees mentioned above. Additionally, in 2009, Caspian helped incubate the Indian School Finance Company for one of its limited partners, Gray Ghost Ventures, which pioneered lending to affordable private schools and in 2016 invested in Veritas Finance, a micro and small enterprise finance start-up. Three portfolio companies – Ujjivan, Equitas, and Janalakshmi – that started out as non-banks subsequently transformed into small finance banks, via a differentiated bank licence issued by the Reserve Bank of India (RBI) in 2016–2017, and focused on financial inclusion.

In short, over the last 15 years Caspian has, through its equity investments, played the role of a catalyst and growth partner to a variety of pioneering financial institutions in microfinance, affordable housing finance, affordable private school finance, and micro and small enterprise finance.

As an impact-driven equity investor, Caspian looks for certain pre-requisites in the sectors it invests in:

- An addressable market opportunity, focused on underserved customers: sizeable customer demand and a viable business model to meet it.
- Favourable macros: regulatory clarity and support, assessable risks and mitigants, availability of resources.
- Quality of promoters: interest from promoters with experience and some domain expertise; intent and motivation to focus on the underserved market.

In 2007–2008, when the idea of the IFIF was taking shape, Caspian conducted an evaluation of the landscape that existed at the time. Based on the results, it felt positive about the affordable housing finance opportunity on most of the above parameters.

Financing Caspian's housing portfolio

At the time of that initial research on housing, Caspian was open to the idea of encouraging MFIs to add housing finance to their offering. However, it became apparent early on that most MFIs lacked the required expertise and the structure to address the opportunity. Significant changes were required in human resources, sales and distribution strategy, systems, and type of debt funding to diversify into housing. Also, their hands were full: microfinance offered a huge opportunity and most MFIs, barring a few exceptions, wanted to pursue that opportunity single-mindedly. Those that added housing microfinance to their product mix had their options substantially narrowed by the regulations enacted following the Andhra Pradesh crisis in 2010. Either they had to restrict their housing loans to 15 per cent of total portfolio, or otherwise had to force-fit housing products to match the Reserve Bank of India's criteria for microcredit, which was overly restrictive for this purpose.

While MFIs provided limited opportunities for investing in housing finance, the new breed of A-HFCs proved ideal (see the India deep dive in Chapter 2 for more detail). These start-ups, focused on micro-mortgages, offered a compelling way for Caspian to invest in affordable housing finance. Its first investment in an A-HFC was made in 2009, to the Micro Housing Finance Corporation (MHFC). Over the next three years, Caspian supported the setting up of Equitas Housing Finance (2011), a wholly owned subsidiary of an existing Caspian MFI investee, Equitas Holdings. This was followed by an investment in Aptus Value Housing Finance (2012). Another Caspian investee, Ujjivan Financial Services, launched housing microfinance for its microfinance borrowers in 2012 and added micro-mortgages as a separate vertical business in 2014. Other Caspian MFI investees also launched housing finance pilots, but these remained small and did not scale up.

Each of these three A-HFCs – MHFC, Aptus, and Equitas Housing Finance – has a unique approach to offering micro-mortgages that sets them apart from each other. MHFC followed a project-led model, providing loans for purchase of housing units in medium- to large-sized projects (100+ units per project) by developers who cater to low income (EWS and LIG) customers.[12] Aptus invested in a strong branch distribution network to reach customers in small towns and cities, catering primarily to the self-construction market.[13] Equitas offers both project-based and self-construction loans and, following its conversion to a small finance bank (SFB), has further broadened its customer base to include a wider income spectrum.

Caspian's investments in A-HFCs, especially Aptus and MHFC, were part of a deliberate strategy to back companies/promoters who would provide a variety of housing finance solutions to underserved customers based on what was relevant in their local area, met the needs of target customers, and did so at an affordable price point. MHFC's project-led model was the most relevant product for the western states in which it operated; the pricing of its loans was kept low, with a view to meet the affordability levels of their EWS and LIG customers. Likewise, Aptus's focus on the southern region and a slightly higher income segment of LIG and MIG (middle income group) borrowers with informal incomes, penetrated a different unserved market that required a deeper physical distribution network and consequently had higher costs. The demand for self-construction loans in this geography/segment is high, while price sensitivity is relatively low. Most Aptus customers are micro and small entrepreneurs who often need business loans too, which Aptus was also able to offer seamlessly to this segment, in addition to housing loans.

Caspian exited Equitas in 2016 through an IPO sale, MHFC in 2018 through a trade sale, and Aptus in 2019 through a secondary sale. All these investments have yielded the fund very attractive returns. On a cumulative basis, Caspian invested USD 15.8 million and has achieved a gross exit of USD 66 million from its AHF companies.[14]

Risks in affordable housing finance

For an equity investor in 2008–2009, risk had to be assessed at two levels: the viability of the business idea, since it was untested, and the implementation risk. The business model for affordable housing finance assumed that the credit behaviour of these portfolios would be similar to that of mainstream housing finance portfolios: low gross non-performing assets and high recovery rates. Except for interest rates, the product features of housing microfinance and micro-mortgages were similar to the standard market offering to high income customers. The key challenge in affordable housing finance was the assessment of income and its variability, for which methods had to be developed and a higher provision for credit risk had to be made. This translated into higher net interest margins in the product design. Current interest rates in housing microfinance and micro-mortgages are between 200 and 500 basis points (bps) higher than what is presently available for mainstream housing loans.[15]

The credit data available on A-HFCs shows that this theory has held up. There are some outliers, at both ends of the spectrum, but by and large the A-HFC non-performing assets are higher by ~100 bps, which means that gross delinquencies may be higher by ~300 bps, compared to HFCs serving middle- and upper-income clients. This level of increased risk is adequately covered by the higher net interest margins of affordable housing finance portfolios.

The implementation risks for affordable housing finance include:

- Availability of long-term liabilities to fund a long-term loan book, especially micro-mortgages, where contractual loan tenors are as high as 15 years or more: this aspect was untested at the time Caspian first invested in housing finance. Micro-mortgage portfolios did not have the blanket priority sector lending tag that MFIs enjoyed, and credit behaviour was still untested (portfolios were small and unseasoned) making it considerably harder to borrow from banks compared to MFIs. The availability of refinance lines from the NHB helped, but it was not easy to qualify for their support and it took at least two or three years of track record to tap that source. In the initial years A-HFCs had to be largely equity funded, with only a few banks and NBFCs willing to lend. After establishing a track record, about three to four years after Caspian's first investment, bank loans started to flow into the sector with some ease and predictability.
- Monitoring end-use: financing a customer who is a genuine end-user is a big mitigant to credit risk in housing finance. Experience shows that end-user portfolios perform much better than those comprising investors, and that it is much easier to ensure in micro-mortgages than in housing microfinance, since the former are typically used to fund completed homes. Regularly tracking home improvement or self-construction projects for housing microfinance enables monitoring, but adds to the operating expense.
- Improper assessment of property value and legal title: this is a key risk in micro-mortgages and requires developing in-house processes and

expertise similar to banks and mainstream HFCs. It is also the most expensive part of credit operations of an A-HFC.

- Pre-closure risk: exercising foreclosure rights in case of micro-mortgages can be fraught with local/political risk. Whether the property in question can be foreclosed or not in practice needs to be assessed at the time of lending.

- Growth in housing finance, especially micro-mortgages, is limited by supply side constraints more than any others. Developers of low-income housing often find it difficult to achieve a healthy return on their investment; many recent projects have not delivered their target returns. A-HFCs that focused primarily on financing units supplied by private sector developers have faced a slow-down. A healthy mix of different types of housing (self-construction, ready property resale, developer projects) in the portfolio of an A-HFC helps to balance this risk.

Finally, there was general investment market risk. Because Caspian's investments in AHF came close at the heels of the US subprime-mortgage-triggered global financial crisis, many of our limited partners were wary of affordable housing in India and feared similarities with the US subprime mortgage business. While we were able to convince them of the clear differences between the two sectors and the products they offer, it underlined the risk that other equity investors may not support AHF ventures unless those differences could be clearly demonstrated, with investees posting strong results in the early years.

Learnings

Pioneers who have successfully experimented with a new idea in financial services have typically come from a related or an adjacent sector, but rarely from the exact same one. This was the case in housing finance too: these early founders showed a combination of risk-taking ability and creativity which was often absent in those who had worked in the traditional, mainstream housing finance sector for a long time. They were clear about their impact goals and the market segment they wanted to focus on.

The business model viability demonstrated by the A-HFCs and MFIs that pioneered micro-mortgages and housing microfinance in 2009–2012 became the foundation for others to follow. They had the advantage of time and space to experiment.

In the tech venture space, it is said, a start-up either gains market share at the expense of others or fades away. It is not so stark in case of financial services start-ups, but they do reach a point of inflection beyond which a venture either continues to grow or stagnates. The reasons for stagnation mostly relate to founders not having the skill or the interest to change and adapt. At times the organization is unable to graduate from a creative, ideas-centric organization to an operations-intensive one. At other times, founders are too slow to adapt the product or delivery design based on actual experience. It is at this point of inflection that founders and investors need to find a way to keep the business moving forward.

Technology has played a big role in protecting A-HFCs from operational and credit risks. Reaching small towns, typically spread over a wide area, is essential to tapping the big market opportunity of serving low-income clients. To manage such an operation for a secured loans business requires robust processes, and scaling them up requires appropriate technology solutions. Inadequate controls can be dangerous, as was seen from rising delinquencies among some of the A-HFCs that grew too quickly.

In the 10 years since Caspian funded the first A-HFC, the nascent sector has accumulated substantial data on credit and business performance. Portfolios have achieved critical size and have seasoned sufficiently to be analysed. The results show a lot of similarity to the credit behaviour of mainstream and AHF portfolios. The lead indicators of good/bad performance are similar too, though due to higher income volatility and vulnerbilities of the borrowers, higher provisions for repayment delays need to be made and priced into the loan. A successful A-HFC is one that has the capability to capture and analyse customer data and use it for underwriting future loans. Data mining and data intelligence is essential for A-HFCs.

There were apprehensions about legal and practical ability to foreclose a security. These doubts now stand dispelled. Not only does the foreclosure regulation work, it catalyses customers to cooperate with lenders and find the best possible solution for all concerned. In-house experience in collecting past-due loans and sensitive handling of customers is paramount for running a successful A-HFC business.

About exits

For an equity investor, the exit – that is to say, the sale of the equity stake in the investment – is the key and ultimate measure of success, at least financially speaking. A quality asset will always attract investors, but the journey from initial interest to an actual exit can be a long one, even for the best of companies. Affordable housing finance is still a small part of the overall non-banking financial company sector. When compared to other inclusive finance assets such as microfinance and micro, small, and medium enterprise finance (secured and unsecured), it is slower to scale, and the net interest margin is nearly 50 per cent lower.

That said, there are several positive features that offset these apparent negatives: affordable housing finance is a stable, long-term portfolio with strong, predictable credit behaviour, and is moreover a large market and with lots of room for growth. And the sector has one additional factor: its customers are more sensitive to high service quality than they are to price, which allows providers to focus on delivering social impact.

Conclusion

From its early beginnings a decade ago, a new sector has taken root, grown, and created its own identity within the broader inclusive finance sector. The future potential of A-HFCs and other institutions focusing on AHF remains very positive in India. Urbanization is leading growth in demand, with key performance metrics and success factors becoming clear, and there is still a lot of room for growth, especially in smaller towns.

The advent of small finance banks is bound to change the nature of this market in the years ahead. SFBs have thus far been busy transitioning from their earlier avatars into banks. Once they have stabilized their resourcing and distribution, they are likely to become a source of competition for A-HFCs. Customers will have more options and there may be downward pressure on interest rates. Well-managed A-HFCs will be able to stand up to that competition and will co-exist with their unique value propositions. Whether the customers are served by banks, SFBs or A-HFCs, affordable housing finance has a bright and vibrant future in India.

Notes

1. OPIC is now known as the Development Finance Corporation (DFC).
2. The decrease from 2018 is the result of two OPIC notes repayments, and the corresponding MFIs' repayments, as the fund has begun to slow down last year and will continue to do so until 2026 when the last OPIC repayment is expected.
3. Portfolio at risk refers to portfolio at risk over 30 days plus rescheduled portfolio or PAR30+resch.
4. In 2019, NHB's ownership was transferred from the Reserve Bank of India (RBI) to the government of India, and its regulatory authority was moved to RBI. NHB will continue to supervise and finance HFCs.
5. Compared to per capita GNI of USD 2,020 (2018).
6. IFC clients pay for advisory services. In certain markets, particularly International Development Association (IDA) countries, advisory services may be subsidized.
7. More than 80 per cent of the Indian workforce is informally employed, see ILO (2012).
8. The IFC was an early investor in HDFC when India's mortgage market was undeveloped.
9. See <https://equator-principles.com/about//>.
10. Adapted from IFC (2015). Figures updated by author.
11. Mona was an Investment Director with Caspian Impact Investment Advisers from August 2007 until April 2019.
12. Defined legally as economically weaker section (EWS) and low income group (LIG). The government's housing schemes define these segments as households earning <INR 300,000 p.a. (USD 4,600), and INR 300,000–600,000 p.a. (USD 4,600–9,200) respectively.

13. Self-construction loans are given for customers building their own house on land that they already own. Loan-to-value ratios in these loans are therefore very low, as land is normally self-funded by the customer.
14. Equitas investment and exit values are not included since Caspian's investment was in the holding company that had several other businesses under it: microfinance, MSME finance, commercial vehicle finance, etc.
15. 100 basis points = 1 per cent

References

CSFI (2018) 'Finance for All: Wedded to Fintech, for Better or Worse' [colloquially known as the 'Banana Skins' report for financial inclusion], Centre for the Study of Financial Innovation, New York, NY <www.csfi.org/financial-inclusion-banana-skins>.

GIIN (2019) 'Annual Impact Investor Survey 2019', Global Impact Investing Network <https://thegiin.org/assets/GIIN_2019%20Annual%20Impact%20Investor%20Survey_webfile.pdf>

Habitat for Humanity (2017) 'The 2016–17 State of Housing Microfinance: Understanding the Business Case of Housing Microfinance', Terwilliger Center for Innovation in Shelter <www.habitat.org/sites/default/files/documents/The-2016-17-State-of-Housing-Microfinance-Understanding-the-Business-Case-for-Housing-Microfinance.pdf>.

IFC (2015) 'Fulfilling the Housing Dreams of Microfinance Clients' in Smart Lessons, March 2015 <http://documents.worldbank.org/curated/en/357431468184465140/pdf/99071-BRI-IFC-587787-SMART-LESSONS-Box393181B-PUBLIC-20150407T143627-2015-Fullfilling-Household-Dreams.pdf>.

ILO (2012) 'Statistical update on employment in the informal economy <http://laborsta.ilo.org/applv8/data/INFORMAL_ECONOMY/2012-06-Statistical%20update%20-%20v2.pdf>

NHB (2018) 'Report on Trend and Progress of Housing in India 2018', National Housing Bank of India, p. 154, table 4.11 <https://nhb.org.in/publications_post/report-on-trend-and-progress-of-housing-in-india-2018/>.

Author biographies

Deborah Burand is a professor of clinical law at NYU School of Law, where she directs the International Transactions Clinic and co-directs the Grunin Center for Law and Social Entrepreneurship. Professor Burand has served as general counsel to the US government's development finance institution. She has also worked in the microfinance sector.

Claudia Rojas is Triple Jump's Credit Risk & Restructuring Manager. She was previously the regional manager for Mexico, Central America and the Caribbean and from this position she helped deploy the funds of the MicroBuild Fund since its inception in 2012.

Mr R.V. Verma, former Chairman and MD of the National Housing Bank, India, held several leadership positions during his 25 years' service in the housing, mortgage and real estate sector. Mr Verma played a key role in the formulation of various national-level policies and programmes on affordable, low-income, and informal sector housing and housing microfinance.

W. Britt Gwinner is an independent emerging markets advisor. Until retirement in 2019 he was Head of Housing Finance for the International Finance Corporation.

Lucie Astier Such works for Agence Française de Développement as a Task Team Leader in Financial Systems, specializing in housing finance.

Vinod Kothari is author of several publications on securitization as well as housing finance, and is a consultant and trainer on structured finance. He heads an eponymous consulting company in India, and has consulted all over the world on specialized financial subjects.

Mona Kachhwaha is an impact investor based in India. As the fund manager of the India Financial Inclusion Fund at Caspian Impact Investment Adviser, she invested in affordable housing (finance companies and developers) in its early days and participated in its evolution over 10+ years.

Conclusion

Patrick McAllister and Daniel Rozas

The past 15 years have seen a remarkable evolution in housing finance in the developing world, from a situation where a poor person taking a loan for housing would be very rare indeed, to one where several financial products may exist for her to choose from. Housing microfinance can take a lot of credit for starting this trend, as the pioneering work of Habitat for Humanity profiled in Chapter 4 shows. One advantage of such loans is that they are well-suited to the do-it-yourself housing approach practised by so many poor households, as described in Chapter 3. Housing microfinance is also aligned with the operations and business models of existing microfinance providers that are already serving well over 100 million clients worldwide. Scaling housing finance products could help improve housing for tens of millions more families and make them more resilient to health and environmental shocks.

An equally important claim to the future can be staked by micro-mortgages that combine longer term, collateral-based lending that was once the sole province of banks, with the small and often informal incomes and remittances that dominate the financial lives of the world's poor. Offered by specialized housing finance companies, microfinance institutions, and banks, these loans provide a path to asset building for those with incomes that would once have excluded them. India has been at the vanguard of this innovation thanks to broad-ranging affordable housing policies dedicated to building an inclusive market. They target the very poor, poor, and middle class, and span the private and public sector. Hopefully, India's experience will prove a bellwether for other markets.

Micro-mortgage is not simply a better version of housing microfinance, nor is housing microfinance obsolete. Both are key tools for providing housing finance options to poor households that fit their incomes, collateral, and borrowing preferences. Still, much work is needed for both to be scaled. While India has led the way with micro-mortgages, its regulations have stifled the growth of housing microfinance, missing an opportunity to serve millions of families. In other countries, reliance on housing microfinance for families with unclear land titles condemns them to slower, more costly, incremental building, even when they have the incomes and resources to buy an apartment or small home if they could get a micro-mortgage loan. Housing finance choices should be guided by the consumers, not by the limitations of poor market infrastructure.

Investors are currently turning the keys that open access to the capital market for low income borrowers and their housing needs. The cases in Chapter 5 provide a glimpse of what is to come. Promoters of large-scale housing developments and financial institutions are coming together to ensure the housing value chain, long fragmented at the base of the pyramid, is consolidated and able to finance the full range of activities necessary for housing: land purchase, site development, construction, and final sale to aspiring homeowners. Whether retail or wholesale, destined for renters or homeowners, there will be more investment flowing to this sector.

Technology will certainly exert its influence on housing finance, as it has on a range of financial services. For example, using technology to track sales data of market vendors and other informal sector workers is enabling financial institutions to build models for loan underwriting. Also, apps such as iBuild described in Chapter 4 connect individuals with market information on housing-related products, including loans, bringing down cost while improving quality.

Challenges

Young sectors inevitably come with their own risks. As the housing finance sector grows, so will opportunities for bad actors to take advantage of new borrowers in ways that put their homes and finances at risk. Industry leaders and governments will need to put in place appropriate financial consumer protection laws, regulations, and enforcement mechanisms to avoid the types of bad practices that led to the collapse of mortgage markets in many countries in 2008–2009. In many developing countries, these laws are weak today, and enforcement weaker still. And in the fast changing world of housing finance, regulators must be on the lookout for new risks and be flexible enough to quickly establish mitigating measures that protect markets and consumers; all while avoiding the excessive responses that slow down innovation and growth, as happened with micro-finance in India in 2010.

Saving and insurance products remain in nascent stages, at least with respect to housing finance. Better opportunities to save are needed to help customers build equity that backs up larger loans. Insurance covering the home from fire, flood, and wind, and also the life and health of family bread-winners, is crucial to reducing the cost and risk of longer-term loans.

Building itself needs to improve for finance to play its role. Building codes are generally not aligned with the needs and capacities of poor households, and therefore don't serve their intended purpose. Improving them and educating local (often informal) builders in better building techniques can greatly improve the resilience of homes and extend their longevity. The models exist, but need to be replicated and scaled up to keep pace with both the rising demand for housing and the risks presented by global pandemics and climate change.

The way forward

Ultimately, a mix of solutions is necessary, and public–private partnerships are the way to incentivize such a mix. A variety of housing types is also needed, from rental to ownership, single-family homes to multi-unit dwellings, and fully private and commercial offerings to socialized housing. The availability of a healthy blend of different types of housing is not only good for low-income families with a wide variety of housing needs, but good for investors too, who need diversity in their portfolios. The experiences in this book lead to three implications for housing finance in the future.

First, developing a healthy market requires the right mix of laws and policies that will encourage all the actors (builders, financial service providers, and investors) to pay attention to the housing needs of the world's poor. The India experience presented in Chapter 2 is one example of a holistic market-building approach, but each country will have to find its own solution. Government must lead this process through policy and enforcement, with an appropriate eye on protecting the most vulnerable, including the poor who have the least to spare; but the rules meant to protect them must not result in their being excluded from the housing market altogether.

Second, housing finance offers a major opportunity for investors to grow and diversify their portfolios: national housing finance entities can channel government funding to the market; development finance institutions and bilateral organizations can leverage their funds by working with these wholesale lenders as well as a broad spectrum of investees; private investors, especially those focused on impact or inclusive finance, can take advantage of the opportunities in housing finance by providing patient capital to extend maturities, and sharing their learning. Success should not be measured solely by the amount of funds invested, but by the ability to catalyse and develop the market. All investors can advance the sector more quickly by collaborating and creating consensus frameworks for how housing contributes to their social performance.

Third, retail financial institutions have to leave their comfort zone and develop the skills and expertise required to provide low-income customers the housing products they need. That may mean learning to understand and assess building projects that the poor undertake themselves. It may also entail expanding micro-mortgages, and using property as collateral while recognizing formal and informal incomes. Technology is already being widely employed by financial institutions to increase outreach with existing products. This can now be brought to bear on housing finance to similar effect.

Recall the stories of Panna and Samita, presented in Chapter 3. Both worked hard to build their homes, but Panna had no access to housing finance. She, like so many of the world's poor, was forced to cobble together resources from her own savings and borrow from more expensive sources when necessary. As this book goes to print, she is making slow progress.

Samita had the good fortune of having a housing microfinance lender nearby and was able to build a basic home, and pay it off, more quickly. Her world is no more secure than Panna's, and her circumstances are not much better. Both women have had their share of hardship. But access to housing finance has meant that through it all, her home was one thing Samita didn't have to worry about.

There is ample opportunity to finance better housing for the world's poor. This book presents many examples, and there are even more under way that couldn't be covered here. But it won't happen without concerted effort and dedicated funding. Housing is at the core of every society, and we must insist that improvements in the way it is funded be inclusive, leading to a better future for all.

Index

Page numbers in *italics* refer to figures and tables.

www.ingramcontent.com/pod-product-compliance
Lightning Source LLC
Chambersburg PA
CBHW070934030426
42336CB00014BA/2677